Call Him, He's Home

A Regular Person's Guide to Prayer

Jim Donaher

ISBN: 978-0-578-75640-0

Dedication

Dedicated with love to my parents, Mary Lou and Jim Donaher. They were the first in a lifetime of blessings the Lord has poured out on me. I know I will see them again in heaven.

"Do not let your hearts be troubled. You believe in God; believe also in me. My Father's house has many rooms; if that were not so, would I have told you that I am going there to prepare a place for you? And if I go and prepare a place for you, I will come back and take you to be with me that you also may be where I am."

-John 14:1-3

Table of Contents

Preface

I joined my relationship with God, already in progress. I was fifty-two years old, and the relationship, which was more of a vague acquaintance, had been going on my whole life.

It's just that I wasn't actively participating.

I began to revisit my religious beliefs early in 2013. I had grown up as a Catholic and been disgusted by the priest sexual abuse scandal, which broke in the early 2000s.

Many of those crimes happened in towns near where I grew up, during a time when I could have been one of those vulnerable kids. In hindsight, I am certain some of my friends were victimized in this. I was not.

The response from the Cardinal, and even the Pope, who has since been named a saint, was cold, dishonest, judgmental, self-preserving, and faith-erasing.

I left the church. Or it left me. Either way, it wasn't that I didn't believe in God — I always did. But I lost any faith I had in the institution and its flawed people who had stood between God and me.

To the degree I had a relationship with God, I thought leaving Him alone and not pestering Him with my foolishness was the best strategy. He was dealing with more important matters. I believed He would be fine with that, even appreciate me staying out of His hair.

Having viewed the church as a necessary conduit to God, I wondered whether not having access to God, in whom I really did believe, would become a problem. It was as though God was only available through the Roman Catholic Church, or God was an exclusive HBO original series. I just had to subscribe or miss out.

I relied on God's all-knowing, all-seeing power to come to get me if He wanted me. Like Mom calling me home for dinner when I was little. But I didn't expect He ever would. He had more important things to do, and I was okay where I was. There was no need for Him to get involved.

I didn't have a sense of urgency, as though I needed some sort of threat to my life to wake up. But I snoozed on.

In late 2012 or early 2013, I read an article about Pastor Rick Warren, the founding pastor at Saddleback Church in southern California. It talked about his journey and the growth of his church, which was one of the first "megachurches." The article had comments from some of his critics and a short synopsis of his best-selling book, *The Purpose Driven Life*.

A month or two later, I read the book. Around the same time, I started listening to his *Daily Hope* podcast.

In his recorded sermons, the Bible came alive in a way I never thought it could. There were so many characters—good and bad—moral and ethical dilemmas, warfare, murder, rape, spying, political intrigue, double-crossing, adultery, lying, cheating, stealing, and as much violence as an NC-17 movie.

It seemed Rick wrote *A Purpose Driven Life* with me in mind. The chapters are short and focused, and the idea was to read a chapter a day for forty days so that a habit of daily quiet time with Jesus could take root.

Rick's teaching removed a lot of the extra "stuff" I had grown up with at church and eliminated the need for a middleman in my relationship with God.

It all made sense to me that God had created everything, including me. God remembers everything and everyone He makes and loves them — especially people who are His children. I am a child of God. So are you!

For the first time, I understood God knows I am not perfect, and He loves me anyway. I learned my weakness requires me to depend on Him. Most importantly, to be saved and brought to heaven when I leave the earth, all I had to do was ask and receive that gift from God.

Believing that meant I didn't need to *earn* my spot in heaven through good works, no matter how many I did. Only one person has ever arrived and left this earth in perfection, and that was Jesus Christ. Perfection on earth is not a worthwhile goal because it is impossible for you and me.

While I am a child of God, and thus an heir to His kingdom, I am not an entitled, spoiled prince. There is much I must do, including caring for others, loving all people, eschewing bias and hatred, generously giving of the gifts I have received, and worshiping the Lord consistently at all times — preferably, with other people. I am compelled to do these things, not as a condition of being saved, but to follow Jesus and become more like Him. My salvation is already secured, having given my life to Him.

In the intervening years, both my parents have passed on — Mom in 2013 and Dad in 2015. I have spent a lot of time thinking about them: the lives they lived, the decisions they made, and how they gave my brother and me an example of Christian living to emulate.

I believe God became more visible in my life to help me understand and be at peace with my parents' passing. Having Him with me and learning more about Him reassured me they were out of pain and worry; lived eternally, happily, and joyfully, and had rewarding work without the nonsense of earthly occupations. He has assured me through His word that heaven was all the good things of life, plus unimaginably more, without any of the struggles that make life on earth so difficult. I believe they are at peace. I believe I will see them again someday. I am looking forward to it.

I have learned Jesus is patient and understanding. My inability to focus was not His first rodeo. So He gave me the idea of writing or typing my prayers. Like all His ideas, this was a great one, as it capitalizes on a skill in which I feel confident.

My current routine is to read the Bible for thirty minutes and then write a one-to-three-page letter to God, dated like a journal and accumulated on a Word document. Besides bringing me into daily contact with the Lord, this routine also provides writing practice and gets me to remember people, things, causes, and other priorities as the Holy Spirit brings them to my mind, so I can pray about them.

If I miss this daily time, my day is off-kilter until I figure out how to get that time back.

That prayer journal is now four documents—one each year from 2017 to 2021. It contains over twelve hundred pages and almost seven hundred thousand words and is the basis for this book. I wanted to share some suggestions for what to say in prayer and how important prayer has become to me. As many humble intentions do, it expanded quite a way beyond suggested wordings for speaking to God.

I want to be upfront and say I would love for this book to be a part of your decision to come to Jesus. I will not approach you in an aggressive, used-car-sales manner, but I want to tell you about the joy and peace I have found as I have come to know Jesus more and more and how easy that joy and peace is to get.

When it's just you and Jesus, and you get to know who He is and what He stands for—respect, kindness, humility, worship, praise, compassion, and LOVE— you trust and believe Him. Your faith grows. Your mind and heart expand—your life changes. You change.

I hope this book enables you to begin a relationship with Jesus or enhances the relationship you already have with Him through more consistent, comfortable, joyful prayer.

If we reduce the emphasis on all the other things and focus on Jesus, particularly if your Christian faith is new, you will be fortifying its foundation, enabling it to withstand life's challenges, heartaches, and disappointments while fully enjoying and appreciating life's many blessings.

God bless you!

Jim Donaher, January 2021

Part 1
Introduction and
Fundamentals

1. What's This Book About?

The purpose of Call Him, He's Home is to help busy people incorporate a simple, powerful prayer habit into their lives and, in so doing, help them begin or enhance their relationship with God.

The intent is to help navigate or remove the perceived barriers to entry that have scared off prospective members of the body of Christ. Barriers like complexity, rules, excess ceremony, and even ideas that conflict with Jesus' words.

I learned in sales training when I was young, "a confused mind always says no." Also, the KISS principle: 'Keep It Simple, Stupid.' So let's do what we can to remove any confusion. Simple is better.

We will remove the excess baggage that prayer carries around, which causes people to put it off or avoid it altogether.

Prayer is your channel for communication with Almighty God. Over the centuries, different churches, belief systems, and cultures have developed many rules and requirements that, while well-meaning, do not come from God.

Rituals, customs, suggestions, and guidelines are fine as long as they do not impede your access to our Lord and Savior, Jesus Christ, who is always available to you when you call on Him in prayer.

The key assumption of this book is there is no need for anyone or anything to be between you and God. Certainly, some teachers can help you understand God's nature, your faith, Jesus' teachings, and God's Word. And while these teachers can instruct, pray and intercede for you, you can pray directly to God. All you need is the intention to speak to Him.

Why Should I Read This Book?
You will learn about the benefits of prayer and some answers to important questions and needs. For example:

You long for connection
Whether we're kids on the playground, students in a class, players on a team or a stage production, colleagues at work, or members of a church, we all want to belong to something. We want to feel less alone.

One thing you will read is how you are never alone, even at the worst times of your life, and you are loved no matter how many people turn their backs on you.

You crave reassurance that we are on the right track
We want to know we are "doing this right." We are especially concerned with this when trying something new.

You will read you cannot pray "wrong" if you are sincere and open in your prayers.

You realize you are NOT in control

You may already know this is a difficult realization. But when we understand Who actually IS in control, and He never gives up on us and is always working to help us, then that discomfort is replaced by the joy of knowing God has the situation under His perfect control. You need not fear.

You are afraid of the consequences of the choices you have made and are still making

Many of us are plagued by self-doubt, regrets, or lack of confidence. We don't have the patience to let situations play out before we're tinkering, dithering, and all but assuring that whatever we are trying to do will not happen. We know we will be the recipient of consequences for the actions and choices we make. And even the best of us mess up—a lot.

As you build your relationship with God, you'll realize God loves you even when you make mistakes, bad choices, and even when you intentionally do something wrong. There are consequences related to the choices and mistakes, but there is no condemnation. When you repent and honestly try to do better, God forgets your sins.

You believe in God and want to get to know Him

When we say we "believe in God" and yet do not "know Him," it's the beginning of faith. You are aware of "someone" being "out there" running things, and whether you know them or not, you believe they are there. This curiosity can lead to seeking God, and when we seek Him, we find Him.

By building a prayer life that absorbs you for at least a little while every day, you will never feel far from God. You will be more and more comfortable talking to Him about anything and everything all day long if you choose.

Then, when you say you believe in Him, you will be more likely to say, "God is my friend and my Father. I am a child of God. I just talked to Him a few minutes ago!"

You read that correctly. You can be Friends with God.

You don't believe in God, yet you're afraid of what He might do when it turns out you're wrong

I am hopeful you will find a stronger relationship through prayer and familiarity with the Lord that will move you firmly into the "believer" column. This will increase your confidence and certainty that you are saved, that God loves you, and that you owe it to those you care about to share this information with them.

In that way, you will discard the need to hedge your bets as to whether God exists. You will know He does, and you will talk with Him regularly.

You wonder how your faith might grow over time as you deepen your relationship with God

As you pay attention, you will see God at work more and more. He's always been there and always will be, but your eyes will be sharper because you will notice His works.

You will notice miracles, both large and small. A flower. A thunderstorm. A child learning to read. Your own breathing. The Red Sox winning the World Series after eighty-six years of failure. The way things tend to work out just like you prayed for.

You stop thinking everything is random and start to consider the various things that had to come into the coordinated sequence to create that flower, storm, child, breath, or championship.

The infinite complexity of God's creation will become more evident to you. You may not understand it more, but you will respect that it is unfathomably complicated and yet works all the time.

You have found lots of books from eminent preachers, priests, biblical scholars, and others addressing this very subject
This is by no means the only book you should read on prayer or on the Christian faith. But it is a good place to start.

It is your relationship with God that you are working on when you pray. As your friendship with and confidence in the Lord grows, your expanding faith is a byproduct.

Many of us were never taught to pray properly. Others were not even exposed to church or religion of any kind. Regardless of how you were brought up, chances are prayer is either a complete mystery or a complicated, detailed procedure with a high price to pay for failure.

The approach I explain here is the one I used to develop my prayer life. I'm sure there are other ways, but I will describe what I have done in sufficient detail that you could replicate it in your life.

It's my hope that if this is the first book you read about the Christian faith, it will not be the last. And even if you've read a lot about the Christian faith, I hope this will contain at least one helpful idea, suggestion, or realization you didn't know before.

I hope you enjoy it.

Who Is This Book For?

Everyone? Well, in a way, yes...

The purpose of Call Him, He's Home is to help busy people incorporate a simple, powerful prayer habit into their lives and, in so doing, help them begin or enhance their relationship with God.

Since "busy people" describes almost everyone alive, you could make a case for it being helpful to everyone.

At some point in our lives, many of us come to where we ask ourselves the musical question "Is that all there is?"

I think a lot of people from many religious traditions are just like I was. Maybe they go to church, but there is no connection. Maybe they pray, but there is no sense of conversing. Maybe they worship but don't fully realize what they are doing, why, or for whom.

Some are too busy to think. They don't budget time that they could use for urgent family or career activities for something the value of which seems nebulous, or at least invisible. They live in the here-and-now, not in the "what if" world of spiritual things.

Some are openly resistant. Maybe they have had bad times and blame God. Maybe they were raised in an environment where God was not acknowledged or even where His existence was denied. Maybe they went to school and were influenced by a teacher or professor who told them that smart people aren't religious or something to that effect.

Still, others are lost. They may have time, but they have no inclination to investigate spiritual things. They are satisfied with their lives as they are. They don't buy the potential for destruction that follows a life of disbelief and denial. At best, they'll joke about feeling lucky.

So, this book is primarily for the busy, the resistant, and the lost?
Yes, exactly. In one way or another, that includes everyone.

Is there anyone who would not benefit from this book?
Realistically, this book may be less helpful for those who have advanced knowledge of the Bible, of worship, or who have a firmly defined approach to prayer for which they are not searching for an alternative. In other words, they are comfortable; their prayer approach is good, and they are happy with it.

The book is for those who have little-to-no relationship or knowledge of God and recognize this as a significant risk.

Or they know a little but don't find the peace, comfort, and guidance happy believers feel. They go to church and/or they say rote prayers, but they don't know why and they see no point. It's just a habit. They are, at best, lukewarm believers.

What's Wrong with Lukewarm Believers? At Least They Believe.

True, they do believe. That is better than non-belief as a starting point.

But being a lukewarm believer may be a trap. Think about other things you profess to believe:

- Science – the earth is round, the moon causes the tides, marsupials carry their babies in pouches, etc.

- Economics – supply and demand, scarcity, marginal propensity to consume, opportunity cost

- Safety – look both ways before crossing the street, don't go outside in a thunder-and-lightning storm, and don't take rides from strangers

- Nutrition – vegetables = good; sugar = bad; fat = bad

You probably believe in one or more of these. You may be a little fuzzy on some of these, but if you are fuzzy on looking both ways, you're going to be hit by a car or at least blasted with a car horn sooner or later. At the moment of impact, you'll wish you had been more passionate about looking both ways.

The same stream of thoughts may hit you at the moment of your death. That is, you'll wish you had been more passionate about looking for God and knowing Him.

That scenario is not what God wants. Not having you in heaven is as hurtful to Him as not being in heaven is hurtful to you. He wants you close to Him so that, at the moment of your death, you enter His heavenly kingdom.

God's Disappointment

His disappointment in lukewarm or little faith is explained in three ways:

God's Love

First, God loves us with an intensity we can never understand. Look at all He's done for us for just a hint. So when we're indifferent, or non-committal, or tepid, it's disappointing to Him. Despite this, He still watches out for us, leading and refining us whether we know it or not. He will not give up.

His Plan

Secondly, He knows your future and how important it is for you to stay close to Him. When you drift, you are in danger, and your heavenly Father wants to save you. So when you say He doesn't exist or doesn't care about you, it's painful for Him.

The Challenges You'll Face

Lastly, it's about endurance: when things get tough — in times of persecution, abuse, warfare, pandemics, rioting, or global unrest (any of these sound familiar?), those with passionate, heartfelt belief are more likely to stay true to their faith. They know it well enough to know they should expect to be tried, tested, or sometimes even broken, in the name of the faith. It's part of the deal, so they don't give up.

If your faith is weaker, less passionate, not heartfelt — that is, tepid, lukewarm — you're more likely to collapse under the pressure when your safety, health, freedom, or even your life is in jeopardy. The temptation to save yourself will easily eclipse any vague faith in a God you only know a little bit.

So, to answer the question about tepid belief; if you are new to faith and interested in learning more, growing, and deepening your faith, then tepid is an acceptable place to start. Jesus is aware of any misgivings you have as a new or returning believer, and He can work with them and isn't offended. He has seen it all before.

But if you stay lukewarm, you're still at risk for problems when challenges arise. And they will.

If you are **any** of the people described below — or if you fit into more than one of them — then growing your faith will help you cope more effectively with the trials of this life while also preparing you for eternal life with God in heaven.

If you are:

- **A Sinner of ANY Kind,** Including the one who thinks they're too far gone to ever be redeemed

- A couple with a newly emptied "nest"

- A commuter who rides the train, bus, or trolley to and from work

- Discouraged

- Confused

- Betrayed

- Lost

- Skeptical

- A student of any age who wants to be closer to God

- A parent

- Angry

- Afraid

- Grieving

- Broken-hearted

- A retiree, finally able to spend some time on yourself

Developing a prayer routine to bring you into regular one-on-one contact with God is a great first step toward that important goal.

People Eventually Seek Information about God

They may have a background in some organized faith tradition and some vague ideas about our creation, and importantly, since we're all going to die one day, what happens after that, if anything? And who decides what happens? And what are the possible outcomes?

If you find yourself seeking more information and you pursue an understanding of Christian beliefs, you may try one of a full range of Christian subgroups and sub-sub groups which have developed in different parts of the world.

Some of us who grew up in Christian churches, including the Catholic Church and many others, develop "rules and regulations fatigue" because there are so many different requirements. Some of us fall away, some just to a neutral place, where we just figure we'll find out when the time comes, others to a more oppositional place, not believing in God or anything else.

Rules, Traditions, Customs, and Ceremonies

After a lifetime of following the rules, we ask why they are there. Some of these rules are truly biblically-based, for example, the ceremony known as either communion or the Eucharist or the Lord's Supper. This was a direct order from Jesus, who, after blessing His disciples at the Last Supper, said, "Do this in memory of Me."

Other rules, traditions and customs were added later, sometimes long after. Rituals and guidelines are fine, as long as they do not impede your access to our Lord and Savior, Jesus Christ, who is always available to you when you call on Him in prayer. Those added rituals, however, are secondary to your one-on-one relationship with God.

Sometimes, these were extra ceremonies, feasts, or holy days. Other times, rules came from interpretations of Scripture that may or may not have been valid. (Scripture is always valid, but the interpretation of it can be questionable at times.) Sometimes, the discrepancy arises from a too-shallow reading or what we call taking it out of context. Sometimes it's taking an interpretation that seems deep but simply isn't there. We overthink it.

Other traditions did originate in the Law of Moses, who received them directly from God. Remember though that the Law of Moses was part of the first covenant between God and Israel. When Jesus died and was resurrected, He created a new covenant between God and His people.

A good example of a ritual that became unnecessary after Jesus' resurrection is the sacrifice of animals to God in the Temple. Since Jesus became the perfect sacrifice to God for our sins, there was no further need to sacrifice animals, or grain, incense, perfume, or wine.

Regardless of the intention or origin of these added elements, in the new covenant, we received permission from Jesus to pray directly to the Father just as He did. There is no need for go-betweens such as priests, or ritual cleansing, or specific words, songs, or anything else. Those things are fine so long as they don't act as an obstacle in your regular communication with God.

Removing Barriers

The intent of the book is to lower the perceived barriers to entry that have scared off prospective members of the body of Christ. Barriers like complexity, non-biblical rules, excess ceremony, and even ideas that conflict with Jesus' words. To strip down the process to its essential elements so that we might start or grow our relationship with God.

Readers need to know this is not the "be-all, end-all" prayer book. It is not an academic study of prayer or a scholarly biblical volume. Brilliant, inspired people have labored lifetimes to create such books, and they have the academic credentials and gravitas to do that.

I have neither exceptional academic credentials nor anything approaching gravitas. I am a believer — a child of God. No more. No less.

The idea is to remove the "excess baggage" that prayer carries around, which causes some people to put it off or avoid it.

Prayer is the Channel

Prayer is your channel for communication with God. Think of it as calling Him on the phone to check in. He is always home and always ready to devote time to you.

The foundation of this book is there is no need for anyone or anything between you and God. Certainly, priests, theologians, parents, and teachers can help you understand God's nature, your faith, its teachings, and its writings. But you don't need them to pray. All you need is the intention to speak to Him.

What Would Jesus Do?

A few years ago, WWJD bracelets made the rounds, particularly among young Christian people. WWJD stands for "**W**hat **W**ould **J**esus **D**o?" and the bracelets reminded us to respond in all situations as we believe Jesus would: with patience, mercy, kindness, and love.

Jesus accepted all people, regardless of their past. The Jewish leaders criticized Him for spending time with sinners (tax collectors, prostitutes, thieves, and so forth). Jesus told them He came to save the sinners.

He loved everyone, even if He conflicted with them. Even the men who were crucifying Him were forgiven.

Jesus said, "Father, forgive them, for they do not know what they are doing." And they divided up his clothes by casting lots.

Luke 23:34 NIV

He performed miracles, healed sick people, taught us how to live together in a holy way, and then, in a final act of mercy and love, allowed Himself (His God-perfect, almighty self!) to be killed like a criminal—a sacrifice for the sins of the world, including mine and yours.

> *Greater love has no one than this: to lay down one's life for one's friends.*
>
> *John 15:13 NIV*

And then, three days later, He even defeated death by rising from the dead.

It is this grace, humility, and sacrifice that people miss if they are too quick to dismiss Christians as political operatives and closed-minded ideological zealots. Because God is love, love is Jesus, and Jesus is God.

When you know Jesus Christ, the Son of God, the One who lived among people as a man, you cannot help but love Him and respect what He did for everyone, including you and me.

What Is the Most Important Thing I Should Learn from Reading It?

There are two things:

1. That prayer enables you to do everything you can for God, just as it reminds you God does everything for you.

2. Also, that prayer is not complicated. It *really* isn't.

Because even though the world is an inconceivably complex system of systems... of systems, your relationship with God is binary. Either you can...

Accept the gift of eternal life
(Which comes with no-strings-attached, which you did nothing to earn, but is a demonstration of God's love. You cannot lose this gift once you accept it. Your gift was bought and paid for by Jesus Christ, the Son of God, and the perfect sacrifice for the sins of all humankind, *including yours*.)

Or you can...

Choose some other direction
(Tell God, "No, thanks anyway, I'm good." Even if you make this choice, God will not give up on you — the door is always open if you have a change of heart. God holds out hope you will accept His gift at some point as your earthly life continues. But it's always your choice.)

There is no third option
Either you accept His love, or you don't. **It's up to you.**

He wants you to be in heaven after your life on earth to live eternally with Him.

How Simple Is It To Let Jesus Into Your Life?
You can make this decision by saying from your heart that you want Jesus to come into your life and be a part of you. **This is all you need to do.**

Committing to Jesus is easy, and what makes it easy is you can do this — *the most important thing you can do in your life* — **by saying a simple prayer!**

> *Lord, I don't understand it all, but I know I need You in my life. Please come into my life and help me. In Your name, I pray, AMEN!*

If you said this prayer, or some version of it, from your heart, God heard it, and He is thrilled by your decision. And you will be, too, even if you were hesitant.

See Appendix 5 for more ways to pray for salvation

What Is Prayer?

Prayer is the way to a close, personal friendship with God, the Creator of the universe and everything in it, including you. It is an honest, two-way conversation with the Lord.

God created you and me and everyone and everything else. And that would be impressive enough. But He also created the world, the heavens and the earth, and the universe. Everything that exists comes from God.

And yet, despite what sounds like a truly busy existence, God will make time to hang out with you and me and every other person in the world. Why? Because He created us to love us, and He *does* love us. And He hopes we will love Him back. He wants you to want to be close to Him, but He won't force you.

That said, He is our heavenly Father. He loves you like the best possible human father and then much, much more.

He has known you since before He created the earth. He knew His plans for you to live, what you would do, and who you would know and love. He selected your family as the ideal place for you to begin your earthly life.

Like an earthly father, God wants His children to be happy. He wants them to be successful in their pursuits in life, from finger painting to designing a space shuttle to Mars. From theater camp to Broadway. From tee-ball to the Major Leagues. From counting blocks to graduating from engineering school.

God shaped you for your specific purpose, as outlined in Rick Warren's life-changing book, *The Purpose Driven Life*. God crafted you with talents, skills, abilities, personality traits, physical dimensions, and a zillion other aspects that go into the unique one-of-a-kind person you are to carry out a purpose as unique as you are.

God wants you to love Him, but love is always a choice. For that reason, He does not force you. He does not want to coerce you, nor did He want to create robots who have a default setting to love God.

God can do and be anything. He does not need anything. But He wants to have a relationship with you.

And that's pretty cool.

Some History and Definition

Over the course of human history, people have tried to figure out who God is and what He wants. Religions came and went, or came and stayed, sometimes involving statues, mountains, or other physical representations they thought would embody godlike power.

Some traditions thought God was actually a committee of gods, with various responsibilities like god of the harvest, or goddess of fertility, or god of the wind or sky or rain.

Other traditions worshiped in different ways but until God chose the nation of Israel as His people, the concept of one living God actively involved in the lives of people was not common.

And rather than be satisfied with that level of innovation, God configured Himself as a "trinity," which in this sense means "God, in three persons." Those persons are God, the Father; God, the Son (Jesus Christ); and God, the Holy Spirit.

The concept of the Trinity is challenging, but for our purposes, suffice to say:[i] *All three are God, and God is all three*

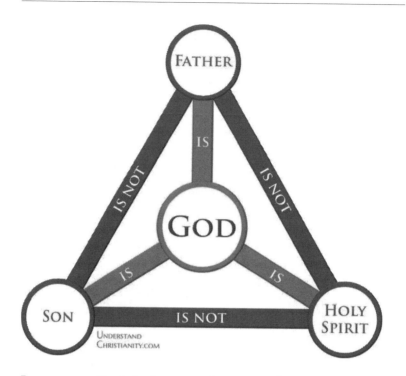

Understand
Christianity.com

Jesus was God in human form so that people could see, understand, and relate to Him. But the primary reason Jesus came into the world was to save His people from the sins that had entered the world originally through Adam and Eve.

This came to pass when Jesus was killed by the Romans in coordination with the Jewish leaders. Jesus rose from the dead three days later. This was the miracle that defeated death and made clear the ultimate ruler over all creation that God reigns with His Son, Jesus, who saved us from the finality of death and instead offered us eternal life.

The Growth of Complexity in Prayer

Like the Jewish religious establishment of ancient times, many committees have gotten together over the centuries to make the rules for worshiping God.

Many of these traditions link directly back to something Jesus, Moses, a prophet, or an apostle said, as seen in God's Word, the Bible.

But some new traditions grew up in various churches and religious denominations. Some were merely interpretations of Scripture that may have been off-target. Others were well-meaning preferences for various types of ceremonies, celebrations, prayers, and so forth. There may even have been some self-serving or destructive intentions for some of these activities.

This book is not the place to read about these things and which ones are good or bad or necessary or not.

But it bears mentioning it was these efforts, whatever the motivation, that served to muddy the waters creating factions and friction that pitted believers against other believers.

The Experience of Talking with the Almighty

While God is almighty, and that can be intimidating, friendship with Him is not complicated. And it doesn't have to be scary. It can be simple and wonderful.

The hope for this book is we can dispel some perceived complexity and mystery around prayer. And prayer matters because it's the most direct way to commune with God, to know Him better, to hear His voice, to feel His love, and to be encouraged, corrected, and directed on a path to fulfill His plan for your life.

Many of us tighten up when we go into job interviews, performance appraisals, when taking tests, or working with bosses whose job it is to pass judgment on us. We also tense up if we find ourselves interacting with authorities like police, the IRS, or some other enforcement agency. Power, for lack of a better catch-all word, is intimidating. Right?

Yes, it is intimidating. No doubt. But why? Because when you deal with earthly authorities, you talk to flawed humans just like you. They may not know or care about you. They may have incorrect information that led to this encounter. You worry you may not get a chance to explain, or the person may not listen.

You may need to convince them to hire you, let you go free, do a service, make a contribution, supply a product, make an exception, or some other thing. The stress is because you may have little faith they will understand, agree, or carry out your wishes as you requested.

Now imagine sitting down across from someone who knows absolutely everything there is to know about you. They know all about your family, friends, and your likes and dislikes. They know where you went to school, what subjects you liked, which ones you didn't like, and which teachers motivated you, and which ones just didn't.

He knows where you are from and what you've done. He knows why you did it. He doesn't misunderstand you. People do, but He knows with total accuracy everything you have done and why you did it. He even knows intentions so deep that you didn't even know they were there. But you must admit they're yours if He uncovers them.

That is what meeting with God is like. You are an open book. There are no secrets and nothing you can hide from Him. It's not because you're too chatty, transparent, or brash. You didn't share too much or too little, mislead, or confuse Him.

He knows you better than you know yourself.

That might sound scary, but it is actually comforting.

When you meet with a human being, you size them up, and they size you up. Two imperfect humans with different agendas evaluating one another. What could go wrong?

Depending on the purpose of the interaction and the roles and goals of the people involved, a lot can go wrong. The tension in human interactions is the result of a complex set of factors, including the size of the stakes, power relationships, leverage, familiarity, level of interest in the result, personal relationships and connections, knowledge, and all kinds of things. Neither side knows for sure, so all sizing up really becomes is a poker game.

But unlike a poker game, where you are sizing someone up who is trying to win your money from you, God only wants to help you. He has a plan for you, and He loves you.

The lone remaining sticking point may just be this: You don't know God.

Some great resources for learning more about God are in Appendix 1

2. Who Is God?

Get to Know God. You'll be Glad You Did.
Knowing God means more than understanding He is the Creator of all things everywhere. It's true and important, but it's not everything.

Another key thing to know about God is *He loves you.* We said that before, but expanding on this, He loves you deeply without exception or condition.

God loves you even if you don't love Him back or ignore Him. Even if you curse Him, He still loves you.

You have sinned in your life as all humans have. Regardless of how "good" you are, you have done wrong in some fashion. While your sins may not make you a "bad person" by human standards, anything less than perfection is not allowed in heaven, which is a perfect place.

God knows all about you and loves you anyway.

There are different ways to get to know God. The primary ones are through worship, study, and prayer.

Worship
This is a big topic, but for now, let's just say attending worship services with a church community when you can be with other faithful people and singing praises to God is a beautiful way to be with God, as He is with you and your fellow believers.

You will hear His words through Scripture readings, sing His praises in joyful music, and hear a sermon interpreting and teaching about God's Word from a pastor. You may also see baptisms, baby dedications, or a congregation member or guest may speak about some aspect of their life and faith.

> *But what about the rest of the week? Can you only worship when you're at church on Sunday?*

You can worship God any time, day or night, no matter where you are. Any time you think about God, He knows and loves it. Maybe it's how you live your life, how you treat other people, or how you appreciate nature, people, or just how over-the-top blessed you are. That's worship, too, because all those things exist only because God made them.

Worship can be elaborate, as it is in many churches on Sundays. But it's just as powerful to look at a sunset and say, "Wow, God, You are great. Thank You for Your magnificent creation."

Study

You can get to know more about God by studying. You can and should read the Bible, which is God's Word, including sixty-six books written by at least forty different authors across fifteen hundred years. Yet the books agree on much and conflict on nothing. Because they are, together, the true Word of God.

The Bible is a great book, but it's not easy. Some areas will seem dull, unnecessarily repetitive, or packed with hard-to-pronounce names. Depending on the version you read, there may be a lot of archaic words that can confuse and frustrate you. **Appendix 1** includes some suggestions on how to find your way in the Bible. **Appendix 2** has some great Bible verses that may lead you into the books they come from.

Fortunately, in addition to the Bible itself, many great books, television shows, audio recordings, and podcasts do a great job of being your tour guide through God's Word. We'll also expand on some of these resources later in the book.

Prayer

The act of speaking to God, in combination with worship and study, is the best way to get to know God, His nature, His will, and His ways of helping you.

You can talk to Him as briefly or as expansively as you like or have time for. You can pour out your heart about problems, opportunities, and worries you have. Sometimes, it's enough to simply give voice to those concerns. Other times, you will pray for answers, people, or things you want.

The Perfect Father, Son, and Holy Spirit

So, exactly who is God?

He is the Father.

He creates, loves, provides for, teaches, corrects, disciplines, tests, prepares, refines, and perfects us.

Although perfection is not possible during our earthly lives, God continually works on refining us throughout our lives by trying us, letting us succeed and fail, allowing us to experience hurt sometimes and exultation other times, and showing us the way a little at a time.

Every time we learn a little more about Him or about the concept He is teaching us, we inch a little closer to perfection. We inch a little closer to being like Jesus, who is the Son of God and the role model for all humanity.

Our lives began before we were born — the spiritual part, that is. And they will continue after we leave our bodies at the end of our earthly lives. At that point, things will get infinitely better, as all pain, suffering, sadness, and reasons for worry will disappear and be replaced by eternal joy, peace, life, and closeness to our Father.

It is this eternal perspective that enables God to take His time as He works to refine you.

Consider how miserable your life on earth would be if you had to perfect all your flaws, weaknesses, bad habits, vices, biases, and failures before you die. You could never relax and enjoy anything.

You would be in constant exam mode, always in the fire, learning or relearning lessons so that you can check that box and move on. Then, when you check the box, you would see the list of all your imperfections in fine print with empty boxes as far as your eye can see as if on a long highway. And you would get overwhelmed. You couldn't go to heaven until you check all those boxes!

Does that sound like fun? For the first time in your life, you probably think ninety or one hundred years is only a heartbeat of time. You would never finish.

Fortunately, and because God's timeline is eternal, He can be much more gradual in His process of refining you. He can let you rest between trials to recover your strength before working on the next rough spot until all the boxes are checked.

Being a perfect Father, God arranged to get you into heaven with a "borrowed perfection." We borrow it from Jesus, who arrived on earth and remained sinless as God-on-earth, yet died on the cross, punished — not for His sins, but for ours.

He is the Son.

As a son, I know I disobeyed my father a lot growing up. On large matters and small, I ignored, defied, or argued with him. Sons do that. And fathers are open to it because fathers are not perfect. Neither are sons.

Jesus is the perfect Son. He obeyed His Father faithfully no matter what the request. His faith and reverence to the Father were total. His Father's plan for Him was to have Jesus humble Himself to live as a man to teach people and then to give Himself up as a sacrifice for the sins of all people. Next time a son tells a father they don't feel like mowing the lawn, think of this!

After Jesus was raised from the dead (putting to rest the idea He was a mere man), He ascended to heaven to join His Father. To ensure His words, actions, teachings, and priorities were not lost when He left the earth, the Lord sent the Holy Spirit.

He is the Holy Spirit.

The Holy Spirit of Jesus lives in the hearts and minds of all God's people. He provides clarity and insight, enables your successes, helps you dig out from your failures, directs your steps, and reminds you that you are part of the larger church, enabling God to work through His people throughout the world.

Like the Father and the Son, the Holy Spirit is part of the trinity that makes up God. The trinity is one of the most challenging concepts to understand, but for our purposes here, there is one living God in three entities, the Father, the Son, and the Holy Spirit.

The Holy Trinity

As discussed in Chapter 1, the Father, the Son, and the Holy Spirit are the three persons that combine to be God. All are God, and God is all three.

It's hard for us to grasp this idea, but suffice to say whether you address the Father, the Son or the Holy Spirit, you are addressing (praying to) God.

What Can You Do for God?

You may be wondering what we, as mere human beings, can actually *do* for the Creator of heaven and earth and everything in both.

In truth, God needs nothing. The list of things we can do for Him is short, but He loves His children, and He loves when we do these things for Him. You can:

Thank Him

Not the reflexive "thank God" we sometimes throw around, like when you get to the movie just before it starts. Do you express sincere gratitude, focusing on God, who He is, and all of what He has done for you? You can thank God every time you pray.

Trust Him

People talk about letting go of difficulties, not worrying about them, or letting them take care of themselves. Things do not take care of themselves. God handles everything, whether you acknowledge Him or not. He will always work out any problem for the good of those who love Him (Romans 8:28).

To let go of things you have no control over — which is most things — is the action behind your trust of God. You tell God you trust Him every time you pray, simply by the act of praying.

Praise Him

Those of us who are overly busy and overwhelmed tend to take some things — perhaps many things — for granted. Family, career, the Red Sox, and your church all get taken for granted sometimes, even if you consciously know they are not the most important priorities of your life. The busy person is more likely to take God for granted. Sometimes, it is an entire lifetime of putting God somewhere at the back of the line when it comes to priorities.

God doesn't need your praise. He can get along without it. He does not need validation either. But praise is a good way to show God you love Him. If you look around, you will see many reasons to praise God. You can praise God every time you pray. He loves you, and He loves your praise.

Worship Him

Worship is acknowledging God's holiness and your decision to follow Him. If you have not yet done so, declaring your decision to follow the Lord is your first act of worship.

You can worship God every time you pray.

Love Him

Understand God doesn't *need* you to love Him. God doesn't *need* anything. But He *wants* you to love Him. And He wants you to know He loves you. And because it is real love He wants, He doesn't force us to love Him. It is up to us whether we love Him. It is the one thing we can give God in return for all He has done for us.

You tell God you love Him every time you pray.

Some great resources for learning more about God are in Appendix 1

3. Excuses, Excuses: Some Excuses People Make about Not Praying

Despite the ease, simplicity, versatility, and power of prayer, many people don't do it. Some reasons people struggle with, delay, or even refuse to pray include:

"Prayer Is a Waste of Time"

When someone says prayer is a waste of time, it signals two things:

- **First,** it says they don't know how to pray, nor do they realize how little time it can take. They may be constrained by some rules they were taught or some doctrine that obstructed their access to the God who created them.

- **And second**, anyone who thinks prayer is a waste of time has never experienced the benefits of prayer. Nor have they been convinced by anyone else's description of these benefits.

You have heard believers claim they can hear His voice, or He's speaking directly to them, and He understands their worries, and He's going to help! They get a dreamy look in their eyes and stare off to the horizon.

So, you try it. You sit, somewhat awkwardly, or maybe you kneel, putting your hands together and looking tentatively upward. You feel a little funny about it, and you try to figure out something to say, but words won't come. You feel like you're by yourself. Finally, feeling foolish, you give up and go on about the rest of your day, unchanged, except you're a little less likely to try praying again.

You might think people who talk about the comfort and happiness prayer brings are crazy. Or maybe you think they are making up stories on purpose to draw in the gullible. Or maybe they are lucid and mean well, but they are trying too hard and turning you off.

Like anything else you learn to do, there are fundamentals and the need to practice. Anything you learn may feel awkward at first, but if you care enough, you try again and again until you get into a groove.

When you are passionate about something, you learn about it, think about it, plan events around it, read books about it, and seek out others with a similar passion. This includes those who know more than you do, even true acknowledged experts. To become skilled, you practice.

I have a passion for barbecue. I am not great at it, but I like to eat it, and I like to try to make good pulled pork, brisket, and spareribs for my family and friends. I'm not an expert, but because of my passion, I have learned a lot. As a result, I'm more knowledgeable about barbecue than the average person.

I have vegan friends who gag at the idea of a barbecue. They might even suggest my barbecue interests are a complete waste of time. I also know people who have traveled the country and the world to sample the best barbecue in all kinds of places. They have spent money on equipment, travel, books, restaurant meals, classes, competitions, and more because they love it. They have a passion that grows, the more they learn and experience.

In a similar fashion, the more you learn about God, the more you love Him. And the more you love Him, the more you want to learn, including learning more about prayer.

You start out joining a prayer meeting at church, or you watch one on television. You pick up an idea here and there, and you try them. Some work for you; some don't, but over time you accumulate a body of knowledge so that if someone asks you about some aspect of prayer, you're likely to have a solid answer. At that point, you no longer a novice. You are helping someone else grow their prayer life.

And the more you learn about prayer and experience its benefits, the more passionate about it you will become.

How We Learn to Pray

For most people, if they have ever learned to pray, it was as a child, maybe as a very young child. My wife and I taught our kids the Lord's Prayer shortly after they started talking. They memorized it and can say it to this day.

I learned it and the Hail Mary when I was about the same age. In religious education, to the extent we learned anything about how to pray, it was still memorization, this time the 23rd Psalm. That was junior high school!

More important than the low level of prayer training we received is the fact we had no idea what we were praying about. Our kids were the same way. We explained some things to them, but they still didn't really understand. This was, in large part, because we didn't really understand either. We thought we did, though, and we did the best we could.

It's cute when you see a small child reciting those prayers. It wasn't nearly as cute when pubescent eighth and ninth graders were doing, essentially, the same thing.

Unless you specifically sought out further information on prayer, or you found a really talented coach, you may still do the same thing before you go to sleep. You:

- Say the Lord's Prayer (if you only say one prayer, saying the prayer Jesus taught His disciples is the best possible one you could choose.)

- If you're Catholic, you say the "Hail Mary." Probably.

- Then, maybe say the "23rd Psalm." But probably not.

- Finally, finish with your "God Bless" list. God bless Mom and Dad, brothers and sisters, the dogs and/or cats, grandparents, maybe other family or friends. And off to sleep.

Why do we stop growing?

When kids go to school, they start in kindergarten. There, they learn things that five-year-olds need to learn, mostly about paying attention, following directions, and getting ready for increasingly serious education. Then they move to first grade, second grade, third grade, and so on.

At each level of education, more knowledge and expectation is layered onto the foundation built in earlier years. Those fundamentals — reading, writing, arithmetic, as well as things like being quiet when you're supposed to — are assumed and expected as you advance and grow.

For many of us, our prayer education stopped before we started school. We don't realize how God is someone you can depend on, who loves and cares so much for us, and who makes a very real difference in our day-to-day lives.

By choosing to read this book, you are acknowledging a need and a desire to learn more about prayer. This is a healthy first step to restarting your spiritual growth and your prayer life.

"I Learned to Pray as a Child. Why Do I Need to Change?"

If you already know how to pray, and you're satisfied with your prayer life and your relationship with God, you don't need to read this book. I hope you will read the rest and share your reactions and ideas with someone else.

Nothing we discuss in this book will conflict with what you learned as a child. It will add to your approach, recognizing that, as an adult, you may want more from your prayer life. No disrespect to anyone who taught you to pray, just as you don't disrespect your kindergarten teacher in comparison to your eighth-grade teacher. Different needs at different points in our development.

My hope is that you will find that it adds depth and benefit, personalizing it for your unique self and your unique relationship with God.

"Who Has Time to Pray Every Day?"

Rather than thinking of it as a time-consuming chore, think of prayer as a new habit you are adopting, based on the recommendations of many, many people over hundreds, even thousands of years. Like other new habits you try to adopt, this one is very good for you, so your comfort level can advance very quickly.

Prayer is something God wants you to do. It acknowledges His presence, which will become more obvious to you as you get to know Him. The Lord wants to hear from His children, just like any father wants to hear from his.

The difference, as we've discussed, is God already knows everything you're praying about. So why bother? Because placing your requests before God shows trust and belief for Him and in his willingness to help. That is why you can ask God for anything, provided it's a righteous thing, not to be used for evil.

When you pray, you must believe you will receive whatever it is you need. You may need to pray about it for a long time. Not because God will forget or purposely stall for no reason. God uses our prayers and the requests they contain to deepen our trust and dependence on Him. He will answer our prayer in His way, in His perfect timing.

Waiting will try our patience, and the enemy will try to convince us that God doesn't care about our requests and has no plans to do anything about them.

Your level of trust will develop over time, and this will be accelerated by getting in the habit of praying every day. God's timeline is eternal, so He doesn't need to rush to do anything. This methodical approach to helping can seem like inaction or disinterest and causes many believers to stray and even to give up on God. Often they do this by impatiently pursuing their own plan to get what they want.

As you consistently pray more often, God will grant you insight and understanding to various aspects of your situation that were invisible to you before. Wisdom is the word that encompasses knowledge, discernment, and judgment.

Later, we will discuss goal setting as it relates to prayer. For someone who has never prayed or who is skeptical about its value, we start slowly—ten minutes per day. The key is quality, not quantity or duration. A good ten-minute chat with God can give you a lot of encouragement and reassurance while allowing you to let God know how much you appreciate His input.

You will also learn that by praying, you are worshiping the Lord who has given you everything. This is not just good manners, but it's also required of all believers to give glory and praise to the Lord for all He has done, is doing, and will do.

"I Feel Self-Conscious"
As with anything new, when we do it, we are aware of being beginners. We are not thinking about God; we are thinking about ourselves. And other people.

Self-consciousness, or the fear of looking silly, is a real concern for people. They fear judgment by others, but they also fear judgment from themselves. As prayer is a solitary act, it is more likely you will reproach yourself than be judged by another person.

That you could be silly for praying is a lie the great deceiver—also known as the accuser, the enemy, the father of lies, Satan or the devil—whispers in your ear.

To defeat this, remember you are a child of God, following the direction of your Savior, Jesus Christ. Let this be your confidence and your strength. Focus on the Lord. The enemy's lies are no match for Him.

"I Have Doubts"

Those who are not fully comfortable with their faith doubt that something like prayer, which has the power that transcends what is visible, could be helpful to them.

It's interesting to note that when you accept Jesus, Jesus has already accepted you. He doesn't exclude or delay you because of your past. And He isn't worried that you have doubts. He can work with them.

So, bring your doubts and questions. Bring your past experiences, your hurts, your disappointments, and your sins, no matter what they are. God knows all about them, and He will forgive you when you repent. For everything. *(Yes, even that.)*

Doubts may start or be encouraged by a lie from the devil, but they may also come at the early stage of your faith journey. Knowledge, together with faith, has the power to drive away doubts and misgivings.

Give yourself a chance to keep growing, keep learning, and find the information you need to feel comfortable. In the meantime, talk to the Lord and get to know what He's like. The more you know, the less you will doubt Him, and you will love Him more.

"I'm Not Worthy"

This suggests God is too great to care about little, insignificant me. It says He has no interest in what I am doing, what my future might be, or what struggles I am having.

You may think you're not important to God. But He went to the trouble of making you. He sacrificed His only Son to save you. He is fully engaged in you and has been since the beginning of time.

You may think what you do in your life is of no interest to Him. You may think praying to Him is annoying, trivial, or pestering to Him. These feelings are unpleasant and feel like good reasons to just leave Him be.

You cannot "leave God be." He is always involved, on all levels, in your life and the lives and circumstances surrounding you. You choose whether to engage with Him, but He is there, nonetheless.

He wants to help you. Why not let Him?

"I'm A Sinner"

Perhaps you are struggling with some sin of which you are ashamed. Given this shame, you think, "Why would I humiliate myself by talking to God, since He despises sin?"

Yes, you are a sinner. You sin. You do it all the time. You do it so naturally that you may not even think of it as sin.

How can you talk to God when you do something He despises?

Well, God made you. He can distinguish between you—whom He created and loves with an incomprehensible power—and your sins, which He despises but is willing to forgive you for because He loves you so much.

Talking to God is most vitally important if you are a sinner. And since there are no perfect people, and we are all sinners, we should all be talking to God.

Don't worry; you will never surprise Him. He knows everything. But He wants to hear from you. He wants you to learn and grow. Part of that growth is learning to own your mistakes and sins.

"I Feel Selfish"
Maybe you are asking God for something that doesn't feel noble enough, the way praying for world peace or an end to famine and hunger across the globe might feel.

Maybe all you want is for the sun to come out tomorrow, so you can hold your cookout outdoors. Maybe you are asking for some material item you really want.

God cares about everything that affects you. He will answer your prayer—no matter how big or small—in His perfect timing. Make your request with confidence, trust, expectation, and thankfulness. He will not think you are selfish. He will know you have faith. (**see also chapter 11**)

"I Don't Know What to Say"
You have heard all the old language words used in some Bible versions. "You" becomes "Thee" or "Thou" and so forth, and all the other words you don't understand. How can you talk to God in a language you don't understand?

This trips some people. They think there is some special 'lingo' they must use, or God won't listen to them. They think of God as an algorithm searching for keywords — leave them out, and you won't get what you need.

That's ridiculous, and it's limiting to God, who is unlimited in every way. God understands any language, thought, notion, idea, or dialect sent through any medium there is and can respond back to you in a way you will understand.

Further, He knows what is in your heart, your mind, and your true intentions. This is what we mean when we say, "He knows me better than I know myself."

The basis for this book is a collection of prayer ideas I hope will provide you with the words you need to get started and feel comfortable.

You won't need them for long, but if not knowing what to say is holding you up, these prayer starters will be helpful to you.

Another reassurance is you cannot pray "wrong." When your heart is right, and your mind is on God, you don't even need to use words. Even if other people wouldn't understand, God understands. He knows your heart and mind better than even you do.

"I Don't Know God"

As you start in faith, God may seem like a stranger to you. Or worse, He might be a caricature of an impression, an assumption, a guess, a rumor, and bearing no resemblance to the true, living, Almighty God of the Bible.

As with talking to any new person, you wonder about the ground rules. Can I get mad? Can I cry? Can I laugh? Is He mean? Will He laugh? Will He punish me for being a sinner? Will He yell at me or embarrass me if I don't pray "right"? WILL HE TOSS ME AWAY?

While it is difficult to truly comprehend who God is and *know* Him, it's still possible to have a relationship with Him that grows and deepens over time. You already know His power and glory are evident in the wonder, beauty, complexity, and longevity of the earth and stars.

But did you know He is your best friend? The one who "gets" you? Who knows where you're coming from? Who cares about the tiniest detail of your life and wants to help you solve all your problems? He is all this and more. He knows you. He made you. He loves you. The more you realize this, the better you will know Him, and the better you know Him, the more you will love and trust Him.

"What If I'm Wrong? What If I Let God Down?"

What if you make a promise to God while praying and then cannot or don't want to fulfill it?

Should you hold off praying when there are obvious solutions you don't want to pursue in a situation? Maybe the hard way is the only way, and you don't want to pray to God to do it because it is hard, and you know He will push you toward that hard path. Your worry that your risk will be high.

God wants you to do what is right. And He will direct your steps toward the right thing.

But He understands you and your intentions. He knows what you're contemplating and has already decided whether it's right or not. He knows what is right, and He will make it easier if possible. Even if it's hard, He will be with you and lead you through it.

But it's still your decision. Realize that God knows a bit more than you do. Realize He wants you to grow and trust Him. Realize also that He already knows how it turns out!

The long and the short of it is this: If you fail, God loves you still. If you succeed, God loves you still. If you disobey, God loves you still. If you follow God's direction, God loves you still. No matter what happens, God loves you still.

"I Have A Lot on My Plate—Maybe When Things Quiet Down?"

This may go along with one or more of the above, but all alone, it is the assumption you will start praying at some undetermined future point. You are putting it off until tomorrow or someday.

Many of us put off complex, sensitive, threatening, or otherwise daunting tasks and responsibilities. We intend to do them, but the time and the mood must be right, the sun must be in a certain position, and it must be a Wednesday and today is Thursday, so not until next week…

Procrastination, seen here with a side of perfectionism, suggests there is always plenty of time for everything. It's not urgent, and we need to do it right and give it the attention it deserves, which takes time, preparation, resources, etc.

Prayer need not take a long time or require special preparation. You can do it, get it done, and get to the next part of your day. The goal of this book is to show you how easy it can be, so you do it more often—starting now!

"I Prefer to Take Care of Myself"

Modern culture, particularly in the United States, celebrates the independent spirit. We consider people who would "go it alone" to be heroes. People who trust only themselves are cool and self-assured. We aspire to be cool and self-assured too!

In real life, none of us is consistently successful when we go it alone. We need other people. Most importantly, we need God. We need to depend on Him for things we cannot control or influence ourselves.

If you don't depend on other human beings—a rough way to go through life, but some do it—you still need to depend on God. Because even when you shut yourself off from everyone else and become a solitary figure, God is still there, working on you and with you.

"Overthinking: What-Ifs, Yeah-Buts, and But-I's"

- **What if...** I fall in love with someone whose beliefs are different from mine?

- **Yeah, but...** that's easy for you to say, you already have a job...

- **But I'll...** never have any friends...

When many of us overthink a situation, we predict a future that is equal parts embarrassing, depressing, unsatisfying, pointless, and sad. In so doing, we effectively convince ourselves that prayer, in whatever form, will hurt, on some level, and therefore, you avoid it.

The last thing we want is to give the reader fodder for overthinking. Instead, enough knowledge to keep moving forward and grow in faith and confidence is all we need.

That said, if you know all you need to know to start praying, close this book, and go talk to the Lord. No matter what, there is nothing more worthwhile than talking to Him. For everyone else, it's great to have you along!

4. Origins of Prayer

Although prayer is infinitely flexible because of the infinite, all-knowing nature of God, there are some principles that apply any time you are praying. They have more to do with your mindset than with any external rules or requirements, as God knows what is going on in your head and in your heart.

The Law of Moses

In ancient times in the nation of Israel, the law of Moses detailed strict behavior codes. The Law included very explicit requirements as to who was allowed to set foot in various sections within the temple of the Lord, how to wash things, how to handle sacrificed animals, what foods could be eaten and by whom, specifics about clean versus unclean items and people, and steps for how unclean people and objects could be made clean again.

Included in the Law were strict rules concerning access to God.

One of the twelve tribes of Israel was dedicated to maintaining the temple of God and ensuring strict adherence to the law, including controlling access to God. These were the Levites. They were the priests of the Lord and keepers of the law, the temple of the Lord, and the ark of the covenant.

The "regular people" feared God. They knew He was with them if they were faithful. But being faithful was a challenge, with so many rules and regulations to follow. And they knew God was capable of great anger and would bring fearful punishment if they did not follow His direction because they knew what He had done before.

On several occasions, the complacent Israelites, having not seen God's fury in a while, would slide away from Him, worshiping other gods and sinning in a variety of ways. Then after God gave them ample time and notice (through the prophets) to repent and resume their obedience, He punished them, using the natural world (weather, insects, disease, fire), people (invading armies, thieves, marauders), and conditions (being conquered, followed by death or varying degrees of slavery and subjugation) to humble and correct them.

Later, having applied His punishment and seeing repentance from His people, He welcomed them back to Him.

Enter, Jesus!

When Jesus arrived, He introduced everyone to the other side of God—the loving, compassionate, gentle, caring, fully engaged, heavenly Father, who loves us with an everlasting love. People loved Jesus, and as more and more people realized He was the Messiah, the Son of the living God, they learned to love God differently and more intimately than they had done before.

Jesus was the originator and perfecter of prayer, teaching His followers how to pray and showing that prayer, and access to God, is available to everyone.

He even taught them what to say. The Lord's Prayer comes from Jesus' instruction in response to being asked how to pray. He granted the people direct, person-to-person access to God by praying in Jesus' name (Luke 11:1–4).

If Jesus had wanted to restrict people's access to the Father, He could have done so, and the people would not have been surprised.

Instead, He made God accessible to everyone, and He went further. In Luke 11:5–13, He not only tells them to pray but to EXPECT to receive what they pray for!

To be clear, Jesus did not scrap the law of Moses. He established a new covenant or agreement with His people. In summary, it was that all who come to Jesus and accept His gifts and believe His promises will be given eternal life in heaven with the Father and the Son (Himself).

Given that as historical context, we realize God is the most powerful, all-knowing, all-seeing, nothing-is-impossible, Creator of the universe and everything in it. You didn't just casually walk up to Him and say, "Hey, God, ya got a minute?"

It's not that God is unapproachable or difficult to talk to. But as you approach the Creator of the heavens and the earth, of all that is seen and unseen (Colossians 1:16), you want to do so with a humble and respectful heart and mindset. He loves you. He has all the time in the world for you. He loves to hear from you.

Having a humble and respectful mindset isn't about your clothes, fancy language, memorizing large amounts of text, or following detailed customs. It is about your approach to the throne:

- Righteous

- Humble

- Expectant

- Polite

- Thankful

- Simple

- Filled with Praise

- Persistent

- Repentant

- Patient

- Confident

> *"Ask and it will be given to you; seek and you will find; knock and the door will be opened to you."*
>
> *Matthew 7:7 NIV*

God wants to hear from you.

If you said, "Hey, God, ya got a minute?" He might reply something along the lines of "Yeah, what's up, kiddo?" God meets you where you are, even if where you are isn't the place of reverence we normally think of.

5. Knowing God

In Chapter 2, we said the three ways you can get to know God better are through worship, study, and prayer.

There are also at least three elements to expressing your appreciation and love for God. While these don't all have to be in every prayer you pray, the attitude and heartfelt affection come out in these ways:

Thanks

In any prayer you pray, you can take at least a second to thank God. You can thank Him for anything since He has literally given you everything you have and has made possible every good thing in your life. You can even thank Him for just being there for you (no small thing).

Thanking Him for all He's done is a great way to express your love for God.

Praise

God is great. And although that is one of the more obvious things you will notice about God, it's still good to make it clear you know it since it's the thing that literally makes everything you are, have, and do possible.

Trust

The third element is trust. Part of praying expectantly is the underlying trust that God can and will answer your prayer. You wouldn't pray and ask Him for things if you didn't trust and believe He will answer your prayer.

By bringing your requests, your concerns, your failures, your embarrassments, and your sins to God, you are choosing to trust Him, which is a personal and loving gesture.

He will not let you down.

While all the details are good to know, you already have the tools to pray if you can put two words together, "Help me!" with the intention of speaking to God.

Having said that, to have a fully-fledged relationship with God, you should know some of His preferences. He has expressed these preferences in His Word, and as believers, we should take His preferences very seriously.

Three important preferences of God are asking Him first before tackling the problem yourself, not getting bound up in telling Him how to solve your problem, and letting Him work without fretting or taking back the problem you've trusted Him to resolve. Some detail on each of these:

Ask God First, Then Focus on the Result You Want

When we are faced with a problem, our reflexive response is to start planning out how we are going to solve it. We think in terms of our own devices, resources, and creativity.

This has a lot to do with the culture of self-reliance and responsibility that many of us, especially in the U.S., are raised with.

God wants you to rely on Him. When you encounter a problem or opportunity or question, retrain your reflexes to pray FIRST, and then focus on doing the work.

That doesn't mean you're abdicating any work related to your problem, but it does mean ceding control over it to the one person who can see all the factors, including the past, present, future, and the motives, interests, and abilities of all the people who may be involved.

> *Rather than pray about the process, pray about results.*

Praying about process, that is, giving God a set of directions as to how to answer your prayer, makes no sense. It's like taking your car to a mechanic and then hanging over him telling him what to do to fix your car. If you know so much, fix it yourself!

The same is only truer with God. As mentioned, God doesn't need you to hold His hand when He works out the answer to your prayer.

So instead of giving God a detailed list of instructions, ask Him for the outcome you want. When the dust settles, and the smoke clears, what do you want? What conditions will have changed? What benefit will there be for you? What benefit will there be for others?

Be as specific as possible in describing the outcome, but don't expend energy on telling God how to achieve it. If you want to add to the prayer, do it by praying for people you care about, or for yourself, or for another problem you need to solve.

As with the car repair example, just ask God to help you get to work and get your car fixed. Maybe He will just enable the mechanic you were already going to choose to work on the car. He might also have that shop closed for some reason, causing you to take it to a different place. You may even think that it's inconvenient and annoying to take your car to a new place.

NOTE: Some will tell you not to pray for mundane things like getting your car fixed, having a piece of apple pie left at your favorite diner at lunchtime, or that your son will have mowed the lawn by the time you get home.

I disagree. I would tell you that you can ask God for anything, any time, and you will be even more comfortable doing so when you pray regularly, praising and giving Him thanks and glory. Not asking him for certain things suggests that you would somehow annoy or frustrate Him, and that is not possible. If you want something, He cares about it and wants to hear from you.

We shouldn't try to micromanage God. One reason is we don't have to. He's promised to answer our prayers, and He is faithful and infinitely capable in doing so.

The other practical reason not to micromanage Him is that while you have prayed for an outcome, it is God's will that will be done, not yours.

The answer to your prayer is interwoven with the prayers and unexpressed needs of millions of people. But He will work things out so that you get what you need, and he wants to hear your prayers. While He works out your problems, He also addresses some skill and character development as he works on the long-term project that is you and making you more like Jesus.

Try Not to Tell God How to Do It

This is hard for a lot of us. It could be considered a subset of the Trust section above or the Let It Go section below.

Having tried and tried to solve a problem using your own power, you turn to God as a last-ditch effort. Maybe He will save the day?

When you've invested a lot of time in a problem, you may have a solid way of approaching it. Even though your approach didn't work or couldn't be done, you feel a need to give God instructions or background. As if he doesn't know.

He doesn't need instructions. Or your ideas or guidance. He knows what you need, and He will either deliver the outcome you want His way, or He will deliver something better than just your desired result.

Even with the time you invested in trying to solve the problem, your experience is no match for God's all-knowing nature.

Let it Go

Having prayed to God with persistence and consistency with great humility and trust, there is something else you need to do:

You need to give it to God and stop trying to take it back. Let God handle it!

If it's not happening as quickly as you would like, it's because the time is not yet right for His solution. Making you wait may have the secondary benefit of teaching you patience, trust, and faith, which is actually a big reason He does anything for us.

As anxious and urgent as you think it is, realize two things: One is that God looks at time differently because He's not bound by it.

The other reason is that He is solving it differently (and better) than you would. On your best day, your imagination is dwarfed by God's universal power.

Sometimes His solution involves some coordination with other events, which He also controls in the process of answering other people's prayers as well as yours.

Another reason you may wish to hold onto some part of the problem is pride. You don't want to appear to have been incompetent, neglectful, or lazy in your approach to the problem.

You want to make sure everyone—including and especially God—knows you have tried, given it a lot of thought, and it's not as easy as it looks.

This is an action that has roots in our human interactions. We've all gotten help from someone who takes care of your problem for you but sneers their contempt in some overt or subtle way. God won't do that. He wants to solve problems for you, and He does so joyfully.

Because He's doing it for you!

Some great resources for learning more about God are in Appendix 1

Part 2
Preparing to Pray

6. Goals for Prayer Time

As is the case with any new endeavor where you wish to establish a habit, setting goals helps focus and measure the effectiveness of your efforts.

As is the case with other aspects of prayer, this need not be unduly complicated or time-consuming. Your aim is to first begin, then maintain, and, finally, to grow your relationship with God. Prayer is one of the easiest and most rewarding ways to do that.

Setting and Updating Goals for Prayer

Your first goal in your prayer initiative is to start. I would implore you not to be overly ambitious with your goals, especially at first, because if you overshoot and become discouraged, that makes it harder.

Starting is easy. It can be something small and concrete, like memorizing the Lord's Prayer or the 23rd Psalm. If you are reading these prayers even for a few minutes a day, you are praying. Just be mentally present and not going through the motions.

Maintaining a new habit may be the most challenging thing. This is often helped by routine in terms of time, place, and agenda. Again, the simpler you make the goal, the more likely you are to maintain it in the beginning when it feels new and unfamiliar.

While it is important to keep your goals simple, it is also key to keep track of when you pray and note any times when you don't. You can just put a checkmark on your calendar or marks on a napkin, but measure how often you pray.

Tracking and measuring are critical to providing information about when to adjust or add to your goals. If your first goal is to start, and your second goal is to pray every day for a few minutes for thirty days in a row, your third goal might involve an enhancement, maybe adding an activity, expanding your Bible study, or journaling.

You can run through your goals as quickly or as methodically as you like. The key is making them work for you as you work toward them.

SMART Goals
Smart goals are SMART goals.

- SMART is an acronym for the qualities your goals should have:

- **S-pecific** – You want to develop a prayer habit. What do you mean by that?

- **M-easurable** – You have a goal. How will you know you have achieved it or are making progress?

- **A-ttainable** – There is no benefit to kidding yourself. Is your goal something you can realistically reach? If not, you're setting yourself up for disappointment.

- **R-elevant** – Is this goal aligned with your beliefs and values?

- **T-ime-Based** – Without a time limit, everything (and nothing) is possible.

Some SMART Goals for Developing Your Prayer Habit

Below are some examples of goals that you can use at various points on your faith journey. Adapt them to fit your own situation.

The idea is to be ambitious but realistic. Your goals are a series of small steps that bring you closer and closer to God. When you feel as though you have reached one goal, set another in the same area to continue your growth:

For Those Who Are New to Prayer:

Here are some ideas for goals for someone who is new to prayer or to faith:

> *"I will read one chapter of the gospel, according to Luke every week, starting this week until I am finished."*

> *"I will read the Book of Genesis by mm/dd/yyyy."*

> *"I will read what Jesus said about prayer, including the Lord's Prayer in Matthew 6:5–13 by this Friday."*

> *"I will find and attend weekly services at a church starting within one month."*

"I will plan to pray daily at xx:xx for at least ten minutes."

"I will decide whether a study Bible or an online Bible website is best for me by one week from today."

"I will select and set up a place in my home to have my daily prayer time by Saturday mm/dd/yyyy."

Important: If one of your goals has proved to be too difficult for you, don't panic. You're not being graded on this. It's for your growth and development as a person of faith. Scale it back and try again.

Also, God already gives you an 'A' for committing to Him. He doesn't mind if you have to tinker with your goals. He is bringing you along nicely!

Goals For When You Graduate from Beginner:
Now that your feet are wet, you can stretch a little.

Maybe you have identified areas you'd like to strengthen or strengths you'd like to make even stronger. The key is to not be satisfied that you are consistently achieving your beginner goals with little effort. If it isn't a stretch, you won't grow and benefit the way you want to.

"I will read and finish the books of Genesis and Exodus by one month from today."

"I will know and be able to explain the story of Abraham, Sarah, and Isaac, the beginning of

the Israelite people, by two weeks from today."

"I will understand the family lineage of Abraham, Isaac, and Jacob, and the story of Jacob's son Joseph by two weeks from today."

"I will understand how the gospels of Matthew, Mark, Luke, and John differ from the rest of the Bible within the next two months."

"I will listen to the podcast, Daily Drivetime Devotions with Pastor Tom Holliday, Monday through Friday starting mm/dd/yyyy."

"I will acquire and use the study Bible, The Lucado Encouragement Bible as a companion for my Scripture reading by the end of next week (mm/dd/yyyy)"

"I will finish the Gospel According to Luke and the first five chapters of the Acts of the Apostles by mm/dd/yyyy."

"I will increase my daily prayer time from x minutes to y minutes per day starting Monday (mm/dd)."

More Advanced Goals

When you have become a strong believer and are comfortable that your prayer life has developed to a point you feel good about, try some of these:

"I will join a Bible study group and attend meetings at least once a month, starting within thirty days."

"I will share my faith with a nonbeliever in a respectful and compelling way so that they might consider becoming a Christian too. I will commit to talking with this person within one week."

"I will join a prayer group at church by the end of July."

"I will organize a service project through church or through some other group to which I belong. I will have a plan sketched out by two weeks from today."

"I will present the plan to at least one advisor (pastor, elder, fellow member) within a week of completion of the draft."

"I will implement the plan and project after recruiting necessary volunteers as soon as possible and no later than mm/dd/yyyy."

For a worksheet to help organize your SMART goal setting, see the worksheet in Appendix 1

Hold Yourself Accountable

One benefit of stating your goals in the SMART format is that when your goal is **Specific, Measurable and Time-bound**, (you already decided they are **Attainable** and **Relevant**), you are able to answer the critical questions:

- Am I accomplishing what I said I would do?

- Am I doing it with the frequency (for a habit) or;

- Am I making progress, and;

- Am I on track to meet my deadline?

When you track your progress using measurable targets, you can make decisions. Should I speed up or slow down? Am I able to do more, or should I reduce my goal to something more attainable?

Keeping track, especially on a written or computer-managed chart, enables you to make course corrections to get on track or it validates the approach is leading to the results you want to achieve.

Push Yourself

There are three schools of thought on the effort level. Only one is valid:

- Go as hard as possible — the rationale is tomorrow is not promised; you never know when the Lord will decide to bring you home to heaven. You should make every effort, every day, to ensure you are prepared to stand before the Lord.

- Take your time and go at a slow pace, like baby steps. The rationale is quality is better than quantity, and your faith tells you that whatever work you do on your prayer life is blessed. Hence, while there is an urgency to start, it is not a sprint but a marathon. Trust the Lord to work on you and prepare you whether your life on earth has eight minutes or eight decades to go.

- A balance between the two.

The answer, as in most things, is **balance**.

As for the other options, going as hard as you can, even if you have a good plan, is more likely to overwhelm and discourage you in a short time.

As for the gentle, baby step approach, this can work if you are disciplined. But easing into this, without any urgency, may produce a weak habit or even no habit at all. To make this change, which has the power to change your life, you will need more passion or drive.

The good news is that although you are beginning your prayer journey with intention, and you're prepared to make an effort, the Lord is guiding your steps. He knew this day would come, and He is delighted to see you making this effort. He will bless your effort even if your time on earth ends very soon.

So get started, but pace yourself. Just as an out-of-shape desk jockey shouldn't start a running program by doing the Ironman Triathlon. Better to start slowly but meaningfully and ratchet up your efforts as you grow stronger.

As with exercise, if you give it an honest effort and you build a daily prayer habit, you will look forward to it. And as you spend more time with the Lord, you will want to spend even more. Soon you will find yourself realizing He is with you all the time, but especially at your challenging times. And He's there to help. The comfort this relationship brings is real and sustained.

If You Need Help, Enlist a Buddy to Help You Stay Accountable

Accountability is critical to the success of any effort to build a good habit. And you may feel fine with your smart goals and your tracking, enabling you to manage your process.

If you worry about your self-discipline, it may make sense to have a partner—a buddy—who wants to accomplish the same goal you do.

The right partner is as serious as you are and won't let you slide. Likewise, you won't let them slide. On days when you don't feel like praying, having another person depending on you is a good motivator.

The risk with a partner is they are the wrong partner. This means they aren't fully committed, and their behavior may give hints as to this. Your past or present relationship can make partnership dicey, as your outside life can encroach on your prayer life. When you're more confident in your prayer life, this won't bother you much, but in the beginning, it can prematurely end your new habit.

If the person you're considering is a friend, and you have questions about how serious they are, hold off on inviting them to partner until you have gotten yourself started. You can take them on later, either as a mentor or a partner, when you can show them the 'ropes' and help them avoid pitfalls.

Reset when it Gets too Easy

Goals are great, but to get the most out of a goal-setting lifestyle, you need to circle back periodically and review your goals from a couple of standpoints:

- If the goal was a one-time task with a deadline, did you do it? If so, give it a checkmark, pat yourself on the back and move on to the next goal. Say the goal was to invest in a study Bible and you did it. Great. But if you didn't, reviewing your goals reminds you to get it done.

- If the goal is habit-based, such as praying daily for a certain amount of time and/or with a set of actions for those sessions. This is a good time to look at your tracking tool, be it a calendar, a spreadsheet, a notebook page, or some other thing that gives you reliable information about your goal. So if you are a beginner and your goal is to spend ten minutes every day reading some Bible verses, are you doing it? If so, great. If not, consider whether it is from some problem with your schedule, your location, the goal itself, or your effort. Then your options include one or more of tinkering with your schedule; consider changing where you pray, revising your goal if it was unreasonable for you, and finding better ways to motivate yourself.

- Do you need additional goals? Are there things you have heard about or gaps in your experience that you would like to close? Say you read the Bible, but your tracking shows you only read Paul's letters to the Romans, Philippians, Colossians, Galatians, Ephesians, and Thessalonians, then you may want to make a concerted effort to read from the Old Testament too.

- How are you feeling about your effort? Are you comfortable with your effort, or is it too much? Sometimes we bite off more than we can chew. Or are you going too easy on yourself, either not reading enough, not praying consistently about things you care about, or some other aspect that seems less than it should be. Consider this when deciding how challenging you wish your next set of goals to be.

By following a regular goal review process, you will refine your prayer sessions, improve their effectiveness, and ensure your growth in faith and prayer over the course of your whole life.

Try completing a SMART Goal Worksheet at the end of Appendix 1

7. Planning Your Prayer Time

The Logistics of Your Prayer Habit

A lot of people find they are more consistent in their prayer activities, especially when they are first getting started, by having a scheduled time, place, and agenda for meeting with God. This kind of structure helps cement the habit you're building and trains your mind to be in the right set to get the most out of your one-on-one time with God.

Like brushing your teeth, washing your hands, or eating a good breakfast, having a regularly scheduled prayer time makes the process of building your prayer habit much easier.

To make your plan more concrete, make sure they consider each logistical aspect, including:

- **When?** Days on which you plan to pray. For most, daily prayer works best. Consistency in scheduling at a time when you are most likely to have this appointment and not get blown off course by something else is best.

- **Where?** Choose the place where you will meet with God. Physical surroundings matter. Noisy places with lots of distractions are difficult. You can do it, but your focus must be better than average. Or at least better than mine.

- **What?** Choose activities which you will do whenever you have your prayer time. Reading the Bible, journaling, listening to or reading a daily devotional, as well as praying aloud or silently are options.

- **What should your mindset be?** This is important in that whatever time you choose to pray, your mind needs to be sufficiently focused, or you won't realize the benefits of the habit.

WHEN: Time of Day and Day(s) of Week

Thinking through the decision as to the time of your prayer appointment is important. There are just a few factors that really matter when you are picking a time:

- Pick a time that you can reliably do every single day.

- Pick a time when your home or office or wherever you decide to pray (we will cover this below) is the quietest and when you are least likely to be interrupted or distracted.

- If necessary, pick a window of time or an "x minutes by y o'clock" deadline, rather than a hard and fast time. For example, instead of planning to pray every morning at five thirty, I plan to pray for at least thirty minutes by seven AM. I know if I start later than seven, other distractions will sneak in and dilute the effectiveness of my prayer time.

- Prioritize this meeting. Put it on your calendar and make sure it happens! (God will be there—He never cancels—make sure you are there too!).

Pros and Cons of Different Times of Day

To ensure they check all the boxes on the list above, many people like to do their prayer time first thing or last thing of the day. Others do different things in the middle of the day. The key is to select a time that works with your particular set of preferences. (God has no preference, He can do it anytime!)

<u>Early Morning</u>

Praying when you first get up in the morning is a great way to start your day. Spending time with God, thinking through your plan for the day, and asking His help in whatever you plan to tackle is a great boost.

The only downside to this is if you don't like to wake up early.

<u>Late Night</u>

After everyone is in bed, things quiet down, allowing you the undistracted mind that makes prayer most effective.

The challenge is when you can't outlast the others in your house and can't get to a quiet place for your prayer time. Even if you are up later than everyone else, you may be more tired at the end of the day than at the beginning.

<u>During Your Commute to or from Work or School</u>

I used to take a commuter train to work. It was the best commute I ever had. It allowed me to sit, uninterrupted by the many people around me, for about forty-five minutes every morning to read, write, or listen to whatever I wanted. I wish I had my current prayer habit back then since it more closely resembled sleep, reading, or writing anything, just like the other passengers.

Podcasts weren't available then, but they are now, and they're a great option too.

The good news is that when you have a commute, you have a prime opening for prayer time. If you are driving, you're limited in what you can read and write, but you can listen to podcasts or Bible recordings, or you can pray to yourself.

The challenge of doing prayer time on your commute is a distraction. If people are talking, or there is traffic, or if you go to different places on different days, you need to pay attention and can't get lost in thought, or you might get lost for real. Having a seat and a degree of comfort is important too.

On Your Lunch Break

Prayer time on your lunch break may be an option, depending on your particular work situation. If you are expected to eat lunch with colleagues, it can be a challenge, even if the time is social with no work going on.

Another restriction can be the regularity or duration of your 'break.' In my case, I usually ate lunch at my desk while doing work since I am an introvert, and the social expectations of eating with colleagues were variable. I did this voluntarily, but some workplaces have the expectation that you will not take breaks, per se, which is a hindrance too.

An ideal situation is one I encountered in my first job out of college. A group of employees, who were all Christians, met together daily at lunchtime for thirty minutes. They would socialize and eat lunch, but they also prayed together, and I noticed several had Bibles with them at the table.

When I joined the company, I was sitting in the human resources waiting room. The receptionist, who I had met during my interviews, was there, and we got to talking. She invited me to the lunch meetings with her friends who prayed together. At the time, I was uncomfortable and politely declined. God may have opened a door for me that day, but I kept right on walking and didn't go in. God didn't give up, though!

Jesus said,

> *"...for where two or three gather in my name,*
> *there am I with them."*
>
> *Matthew 18:20 NIV*

So groups meeting to discuss Scripture and pray together is a blessed and holy time, whether small groups, one-on-ones, or formal church services.

Caveat on your time of day

I am a creature of habit, and the more structure I can create in my life, the more consistent I can be in maintaining good practices. I present these and other ideas in this chapter based on the assumption that you, too, are a creature of habit.

If you can carve out time in a highly variable day and week, taking a few minutes here and there, then, by all means, do that. You have a gift for time management that I do not possess! If you don't need a consistent time or place or agenda to make sure you spend some alone time with God, then do what works for you.

That said, if you are just starting and are unsure of yourself, a little more structure is advisable, just to give you some confidence. You can always loosen it up later.

WHERE: Physical Surroundings

Indoors or Outdoors?
Indoors

The main benefit of having your prayer time indoors is you are impervious to the weather. If you also have it inside your own home, you stand a better chance of minimizing distractions and interruptions. And your travel time is the time it takes you to walk—even stocking or bare-footed—to the space you have arranged.

Also valuable in an indoor space in your home is access to your books, supplies, your Bible, your own secure Wi-Fi, and more. To be fair, this also presents a possible stumbling block since you also have access to your TV, your family or roommates, neighbors, your refrigerator, and other things to interrupt and distract.

Setting Up Your Quiet Place in Your Home

If you are setting up space in your home to have prayer time, you have some control over the environment you're creating for your best prayer experience.

In some homes, there is no quiet place when the other residents are up and around. TV, music, conversations, chores, and so forth make for a consistent din that can be hard to ignore. For this reason, I recommend either the early morning or the late at night schedule options to ensure quiet.

Once you know where you want to go in your home, setup is easy. This is because you don't need a lot of stuff. In my case, I use a Bible app on my laptop, and I type my prayer journal in a Microsoft Word document, so all I need is my laptop. Many people prefer a physical Bible to an electronic one. Those same people often prefer a notebook if they like to journal. I like not needing to remember multiple items.

If you prefer non-electronic tools and have not invested in a Bible as yet, I would suggest a study Bible. The benefit of a study Bible, especially for someone who doesn't use the internet as much, is when you have questions or want some amplification for a book, chapter, or verse, a study Bible comes with commentary and detail from well-established experts and scholars of the Scriptures. Their knowledge and ability to give context to what you are reading can unlock the Bible and improve your experience and knowledge level very quickly. **(See Appendix for recommendations for study Bibles.)**

If you prefer to use online Bible sites, or if you prefer a more standard Bible (without the amplifications of a study Bible), there are many excellent Bible websites that contain both the various versions of the Bible, along with tools that allow easy cross-referencing and comparison. **(See Appendix for recommendations for websites supporting Bible study.)**

Whether you use a study Bible or simply Google your questions, you will have questions, and getting answers to them sooner than later enhances your experience.

Other than the equipment, the environment, ideally, would be as "Spartan" as possible without a lot of things to distract or waylay your focused attention.

The one place you may want to splurge is on a comfortable chair. I have a standard office desk chair that is great for me since I sit at the keyboard much of the time. If you prefer to sit in an armchair, that's great too. But be comfortable, so you don't get antsy before your prayer time is finished.

Outdoors

For some people, being outdoors makes them feel closer to God. One reason they enjoy it is that they feel they are enjoying God's creation more than if they are inside a building built by human hands. Or they relish the fresh air and (hopefully) sunshine.

If you are one of these people, you can do your prayer time outdoors. The requirements don't change, just the location. You still need to be free from interruption and distraction. You still need to be comfortable. When you are outside, you can choose whether to be stationary or if you prefer to move around.

The struggle being outside, particularly if you are moving around, is the variability of the environment. In addition to weather, if you like to pray while walking or hiking or biking, you may be interrupted one day and be left blissfully alone on another. If you are moving about, the ability to read or write will be limited, but you can still listen to a Bible app or a Bible study podcast.

If you like to sit on a bench in a park, or under a tree, or in an outdoor café, you may need to contend with workers mowing the grass, people chatting nearby, or other interruptions.

The best of both worlds — outdoors, but free from distraction — is your own backyard if you have one. Or you could use your patio, apartment balcony, deck, by the pool, or in a garden.

As with your choice of time each day, where you choose to have your quiet time can contribute to the development of this critical habit of prayer. Choosing a quiet place where you're comfortable, safe, and happy is another reason for wanting to do it—and wanting to do it will motivate you to do it consistently.

THE AGENDA: What do We do During our Prayer Time?

Now you're where you want to be. The time is right. You are comfortable, safe, well-equipped. You have a cup of coffee or tea or a cold drink.

What do you do?

- **Silent Prayer** – Some people can simply bow their heads and pray to themselves or aloud any time they want to. If you want to do that, do that.

- **Reading Scripture** – Some people prefer to spend some time reading God's Word to get them into the right frame of mind. The Bible is a great jumping-off point for your time with God since His Word is literally Him giving you instruction and insight through history, poetry, letters, and anecdotes about the lives of many people, most importantly, Jesus.

- **Journaling** is a way to talk to God if you have trouble praying aloud or even just in your mind. You can write about what Scripture reading you've done, issues that you or someone you care for is having, your hopes, aspirations, and dreams, confessing your sins, asking for help, wisdom, or forgiveness, or simply for advice, wisdom, and guidance.

- **Talking, typing, writing, thinking, singing, or dancing**. Whatever you do, do it for joy and for greater closeness with the Lord.

The reality is the agenda is solely for you. As noted earlier, God knows what you're going to say, what you're thinking but not saying, what you're afraid of and what you need. He can handle those and any other topic, in whatever order you present them. He knows better than you do.

So the agenda is to keep you on track, making sure you get through what you want to talk about, ask about, or praise and thank about. This helps me a lot.

And more good news: since the agenda is for you, you can make it as formal or informal as you need. It must work for you — that's the only criterion that matters.

Here is an agenda I used today:

- **Scripture** – Galatians Chapters 4–6 – Paul admonishes the Galatian church that has backslid toward false teaching, endangering their faith with confusion, jealousy, conflict, and division.

- **Dear God** – anniversary of Dad's death yesterday, concern for unemployed friends during the pandemic, concern for a friend facing legal problems, a question concerning Catholicism and whether it is built on false teaching.

- **Thanks** – For letting me wake up today and be able to read His Word and converse with Him this way.

- **Praise** – God is almighty and all-knowing, so I cannot surprise or stump Him. Whatever weaknesses I have, he can understand my thoughts, motives, and intentions. And if I stumble or misuse language so that a human being couldn't understand the point, God is able to read fluently, my tortured syntax.

I tend to write my agendas as though others would be using them, too, as for a business meeting. This is a habit I developed as a manager for many years. It helps me feel more organized.

You don't need to do this much detail, or you may want to do more. What matters is what works for you.

- You may wish to leave it more open than this, so you have room to explore.

- If you tend to lose track of time, you may want to include times on your agenda, e.g.:

  o **Scripture** – ten minutes

  o **Dear God** – twenty minutes

  o **Thanks and Praise** – ten minutes

- You can set timers on your phone to remind you at various points.

- You may, as many Bible reading plans suggest, include a reading from both the Old and New Testaments.

- Add a podcast such as Drivetime Devotions with Pastor Tom Holliday (up to fifteen minutes).

Try completing the prayer habit planning guide at the end of Appendix 1

8. Simplicity Leads to Consistency, Habit and an Ever-Deepening Prayer Life

Simplicity

As we said at the start, the focus of this book is the simplicity of prayer. One might ask whether something simple should take a couple of hundred pages to explain. Fair enough, but bear with it for a bit longer; I appreciate your patience.

When you were a toddler, you started learning to count. Perhaps it was blocks or stuffed animals or little glow in the dark stars over your crib. Then either your mother or father, or a kindergarten teacher, or Sesame Street introduced you to numbers—numerals—and you learned the order.

This doesn't sound complex now, but when you were four or five years old, this was sufficient to challenge your mind, which was not yet saturated with all the information that would besiege it in the next few years.

This critical early education was reinforced and re-reinforced so much that it became second nature to you. Later, addition facts, then subtraction, then multiplication tables, long division, and so on were built on that foundation of counting and recognizing your numerals.

Now imagine that instead of counting blocks or identifying numerals in kindergarten, your teacher taught how to solve quadratic equations, or graph a parabola. She hands out graph paper (with tiny cells) and tells you to sharpen your crayons (black or blue only, please) and start taking notes.

She isn't kidding. Fifty minutes later, half the kids in the class have wet their pants, five are crying, including one in each of the four corners of the room, and one boy near the front is standing on his chair defiantly screaming "NO!" repeatedly.

The next time someone mentions a parabola to those kids, they will need three years of counseling. Why?

Because simplicity enables the unfamiliar mind to ease into something new. Like wetting your feet before diving into the pool, a simple foundation takes the intimidation away.

Simplicity is particularly important with prayer because you aren't going to be tested, and if you quit, no one will mind or even notice. Worst case, you may have to fake it when you visit Grandma, but otherwise, there are no repercussions. So as soon as it looks overwhelming, intimidating, condescending, or otherwise over our heads, the easy thing is just to forget about it.

God doesn't want you to forget about prayer or about Him because He loves you.

This means God is fine with you starting our slow and basic. He doesn't mind if you never advance beyond slow and basic if He hears from you regularly. He loves to hear whatever you have to say, whether it's sophisticated or not.

Since He knows your heart and mind, he isn't dependent on your eloquence to explain yourself to Him. In fact, nothing human is 'sophisticated' to God, whose depth, breadth, and mystery far exceed anything our human minds could conceive.

Consistency

Your prayer place and time should become an inviolable standing appointment you will look forward to most of the time.

Realize, though, that in the beginning, it may not be something you look forward to. The hardest time to continue a new activity and make it a habit is somewhere between the second and the tenth time you do it. You're not yet fully committed, and your mind (as poked by Satan) says you can quit anytime you like.

The trick, in the beginning, is to tweak the things that disrupt you immediately before they become an excuse to quit. Maybe your Bible is new and won't stay open to the page without you holding it down. Or you don't have quite enough room on your desk for a notebook, your Bible, and your laptop. Do what you need to do to rid yourself of these snags. Either spend some time breaking in your Bible or get something to mark your place. Either take some unneeded things off your desktop or move to another table.

Don't tweak the core of your new habit too quickly. The other things are just logistical details, but Bible reading, prayer, journaling—whatever format you choose to actually convey your requests to the Lord—will likely get comfortable for you after you take some time to break in. Try what you're doing for at least ten days before making any decisions. By then, if something is becoming a real problem, you'll know, and then you can adjust.

The point is getting closer to God. You will not understand every Bible verse. Some entire books of the Bible will seem to be written in a different, incomprehensible language.

You may read the same passage ten times but get tripped up on one word every time. This is likely to happen often, which is why a study Bible, either a standalone or an accompanying version, can help you over these bumps.

Long story short, tweak comfort and convenience immediately. Change prayer, devotional, and Scripture reading practices only after trying for a while. You must give it a chance. The wait is needed to make sure you aren't just reacting to the newness and feeling less comfortable than you want. If those are the reasons, they will work themselves out before you decide to upset your whole approach.

Habits and Routines

Consistency creates habits and routines. These are activities and schedules that are unchanging and happen semi-automatically, allowing the pray-er to think about his or her prayers and not about things like where, when, why, and how.

People can develop habits quickly if there is some gratification involved. There are good habits like exercise, brushing your teeth, and getting enough sleep. There are bad habits such as eating or drinking excessively, using narcotic drugs improperly, or binge spending.

Whether you or I "get" the allure of a particular habit or not, it provides some sort of gratification to the person who has it—a fit body, healthy teeth, or alertness and energy for the good habits. A lessening of pain is often the gratification of bad habits, although one can also do too much of a good habit and end up with negative outcomes.

Prayer is a habit that brings both short- and extremely long-term gratification. When you draw closer to God in prayer, you will improve your relationship with Him. The more you pray, the more you will understand Him and realize what sorts of decisions He blesses, leading you to make better decisions.

You will see right and wrong more clearly when you look through the lens of God's Word. When your relationship with God is good and growing, your relationships with other people improve too, as you increasingly 'do unto others as you would have them do unto you.'

These benefits are short-term. It may not be today or this week that you realize them. That depends on how quickly you incorporate prayer into your routine. But if you do it, you will get those benefits in time to do well with them in your life on earth.

But as good as those shorter-term benefits are, the long-term (that is, eternal) benefits are even better. By having a close relationship with God, talking to Him regularly, understanding Him, and knowing what his priorities are, you become God's friend. You become like Abraham or David in the Bible, the former being God's friend and the latter being "a man after (God's) own heart."

Neither Abraham nor David was perfect. They were infected with the sin of the world just as you and I are. But they did their best to listen and obey the Lord, and when they made mistakes and committed bad sins, they confessed and apologized to the Lord. Because they did, they were forgiven their sins. Just as we will be forgiven ours.

Ever-Deepening Prayer Life

Think about your deepest, most satisfying relationship. Someone who you are just always in sync with. You think it, they say it, or vice versa. You have a history together, understand implicitly what would help, what would hurt, and you supply each other with help every time.

How did it get to be so deep and satisfying? Was it just immediately that way right after you met?

For God, that's how it was when He created you. He loved you immediately and understood you completely as His unique work of art, His masterpiece, His pride and joy. Throughout your lifetime, His love never wavers, and He urgently wants you to come to get to know Him better.

In the meantime, God supplies all that you need, and He protects you from the dangers of a world polluted by sin. Yet, rather than making you a robot who does everything the master says without exception, God gave you the gift of free will. The ability to choose and do whatever you like. The only limitation is not from God but from earthly consequences.

What God is hoping for is you recognize how blessed you are and seek Him. An innocuous question like, "How did I get so lucky?" could be the beginning of seeking Him. And the Bible tells us if we seek Him with our whole heart, we will find Him.

As with human relationships, it's not always smooth in the beginning. You aren't yet comfortable, and even though God is comfortable, you will be focused on yourself and won't notice.

You'll start to notice that in some way, seemingly unrelated things are linked. You will gradually lessen and then eliminate the attribution of events to luck, chance, or some other cosmic mistake. Miracles, created specifically by God, will seem less unusual; they won't all be huge—some are barely noticeable. But they are all God's work.

Over time, you will become increasingly aware of the ways that God affects your day-to-day life. How He helps you in difficulties and provides you with joy and sustenance. You'll see that some of your friends, family, and even some strangers were sent by Him to help you. It is your AWARENESS of His involvement in your life that deepens your prayer life and your relationship with Him.

As you maintain and deepen your prayer life and your relationship with God, you will consistently be amazed at how much He does for you. And how powerful He is. And how gentle and loving. And patient, forgiving, and caring.

God, you will come to find, will be there helping in every critical moment of your life, whether you acknowledge Him or not. He was there with you before you were born and every day since.

And He asks only that you accept His love and invite Him into your life. If you do that, He will clean up the messes, teach you how to avoid them in the future, and continue loving you even when you sin and fall short of His perfect standards.

Mental Preparation to Approach God

Focus
Clear your mind – Be Here, With God, Now

This can be a challenge. As a lifelong sufferer with ADHD (Attention deficit hyperactive disorder), my mind can wander miles before I even know it's gone. For this reason, silent prayer has always been challenging for me.

This example gives some idea of how my brain works when it's supposed to be praying silently:

"Our Father, who art in heaven, hallowed be thy name...

Wait, "hallowed?" What is "hallowed"? Is it like Halloween? Anyway...

Our Father, who art in heaven, hallowed be thy name. Thy kingdom come...

Shouldn't there be a comma there? I thought Luke was a doctor. Doesn't he know punctuation?

I bet he wishes he had someone proofread his Gospel for him. He had no idea how many readers he might have...

Readers...how many? What if he had a revenue stream from that? Would it be in shekels?

"Thy kingdom come, thy will be done on earth...

If he was a doctor, why was he wandering around writing biblical history?

History. I had such a crush on my eighth-grade history teacher, Ms. Arvendale. I wonder whatever happened to her...She'd have to be in her late '70s..."

And so on, until I was in the basement, searching for my junior high yearbook, getting distracted by the mess and the need to clean it up, and before too long, I forgetting all about praying.

Whether you're clinically diagnosed with attention issues or not, I suspect distraction plagues a lot of people who might otherwise have active prayer lives.

Distraction – A Tool for God to Use in Refining You

God made you, and He knows how you are. Distraction may be a way of testing and refining you, as He does with all of us. If you don't pray, God doesn't just throw up His hands and say, "Oh, well, not gonna happen." He continues to work on you.

It may be that He is allowing these distractions to see how you react to them. He did this with me for many years, and I didn't do anything about it. I must confess that it didn't really matter that much to me.

Time after time, though, when there was praying to be done, whether in church, in some work situation, or even in a hospital with myself or a loved one as the patient, I would offer some vague plea, *"God... help us. If... You can. Please. Okay, thanks."*

There was usually some stimulus, valid or invalid, that would pull my mind off the prayer. But at least I tried. That was progress, from God's perspective.

Eventually, through a series of faith provoking events, I got serious about prayer. I feel blessed and thank the Lord for his patient, persistent work in developing this aspect of me.

The Enemy = Satan

God also knows Satan and how he seeks to distract, delay, and ruin our efforts to build and maintain our close relationship with the Lord.

It won't work if we are persistent, but it's enough to make us feel squeamish about whether we're really in touch with God and He with us. We can then get discouraged and drift away.

This would be especially risky for those who are new to prayer. One key aim of this book is to get you past that point, so you can see Satan coming and take evasive action, particularly around distraction and delay.

Whether you pray to yourself or even out loud without any problems with great focus, the key is finding a way to commune with God in a way that enables you to be comfortable, open, and honest.

For me, this is accomplished through journaling. Every day, I write a letter to God. Some days I don't have a lot to say. Other days I can write five pages without stopping. The byproduct of this is I have a record. I can go back to any point and look at what I was journaling/praying about.

Journaling also serves as a jumping-off point for a lot of my other writing. I used to fret if I didn't have anything to say, but since I've been doing it for a while, I know something will come to me tomorrow or the next day if there isn't much to discuss today. (There is always thanks and praise, however).

When you pray, you are telling God you love Him, but also you trust Him. In fact, God already knows what you need. And He's already putting a plan into motion to make sure you get it. But He loves to hear from you, get your reactions to things, and give you impressions through His Word and your own mind as to what He thinks. God delights in you because He made you to love you. And He does.

All of this happens best when you are focused. Not on Luke's literary skills and eighth-grade history, but on your conversation with the Lord, who, despite having all of creation to care for, his attention during your prayers is completely on you.

If you find your mind wandering...

- Sometimes, you're tired, worried, or sick, and your focus isn't there.

- God knows before you do.

- You need not belabor the activity just to say you did it.

- God appreciates your effort.

Quality over Quantity

Some people pray for an hour or more every day. Some pray ten minutes every couple of days. Which one is closer to God?

Our "more is better" culture would lead us to say the person who prays more is closer to God. And they may be. Only God knows that.

But it may not be if the time spent by the person who prays longer is wasted with prayer that has no meaning to the person. Or worse, they are spending the time because someone told them they must do that to get to heaven.

Similarly, someone who prays for just a few minutes when they think of it is not likely to 'think of it' very often.

The critical matter is not time, just as it is not pretty words, fancy clothes, elaborate ceremonies, or hollow platitudes that the person doesn't mean or feel. God would rather have two minutes of undistracted relationship with you than two hours of sitting watching you recite words or read passages with no interest in learning what His Word means or whether you really have a relationship with Him.

You can pray:

- in the morning

- at noon

- at night

- at home

- or somewhere else

- indoors

- outdoors

- with a physical Bible or an app

- highly structured

- free-form

- Whether

- out loud

- silently

- in writing

- in mime

- in gesture

- in Morse code

- in interpretive dance

Whatever way you pray, pray with your whole heart and whole mind, whether it's for two minutes, two hours, or two days.

Part 3
Praying for People

9. What Does it Mean to Pray for Someone?

Praying for Ourselves and Others

Very often, when we think of praying, it's in response to some urgent need that either you or someone else has for which they need all the help they can get.

The need usually relates to someone's health or safety, either or both of which are in immediate jeopardy.

When you pray for someone, you are petitioning God, who makes all things and has all power, to help that person with whatever they need, with confidence that He will provide the perfect resolution at the perfect time.

As a believer who prays sincerely and with expectation, your prayer is always answered. The issue may not be resolved as you have requested, but we must trust the Lord to deliver, at least as good, if not better, in His perfect timing.

Although prayer is always needed in life-or-death crises, it's needed at other times too. Maybe a child is struggling in school, a spouse is having trouble at work, or a friend's marriage is breaking up. Maybe someone is down about some disappointment that doesn't threaten them physically, but it makes them sad just the same.

By the same token, prayer is just as necessary when things go well. We are created in God's image. Would we want to hear from our kids only when things go wrong? (I know most of us do, but do we WANT to?) No, we wouldn't, and although God is more patient than the best parents in all creation, he'd still like some good occasionally.

So we thank God for our son's being chosen to play varsity basketball. We thank Him for our daughter getting a big role in the school play. We thank Him for bringing a romance into our lives, a new home, or a new baby.

Life is full of good things. Some days more than others, but they are there. Just as we ask God for what we need, we should also thank Him for what He has already done and praise Him for who He is.

Love Your Neighbor as Yourself

One day, Jesus answered a question about which of the Ten Commandments was the most important by adding two more.

Rather than choosing from among the ten, He added,

> *"Love the Lord, your God with all your heart..."*
> *and "Love your neighbor as yourself"*
>
> *(Matthew 22:36–40, Mark 12:30–31, Luke 10:27).*

His rationale was that by keeping these two commandments, you were naturally keeping the other ten. It also focuses our attention much more keenly on what matters most: Love for God, and each other.

Jesus taught us that praying for someone is an act of love. Advocating to God on behalf of someone in need is a beautiful expression of your love for that person and your love AND trust for God.

Defining Love

Before we identify our neighbors, what did Jesus mean by "love" your neighbor? What may constitute acts of love? Here are just a few examples:

- Helping a neighbor clean up after a storm wrecks their yard or house

- Watching someone's house while they are away on vacation

- Bringing flowers to a new mom struggling with post-partum depression

- Giving money, food, or time to a homeless person

- Driving out of your way to drop off a friend who has had too much to drink

- Donating money or time to a charity organization

- Serving meals at a homeless shelter

- Donating blood or blood platelets

- Holding a door for someone

- Letting someone go ahead of you in line in traffic or at the grocery store

- Taking a picture of a group of tourists, so the whole group can be in the picture

- Sitting with a friend in the waiting room while a loved one is in surgery

- Driving an elderly neighbor to a medical appointment or the grocery store

- Volunteering to tutor an adult in reading

- Sincerely encouraging someone who has lost a relationship, a job, a friend, or some other valuable thing.

- Praying for someone

Any time you give freely of yourself in the service of another person or group of people, you are showing love. In any situation, what constitutes an act of love depends on what is happening. That is, you show your love by fulfilling a specific need for the situation.

Who Is My Neighbor?

In using the word *neighbor*, Jesus did not intend to be exclusive. When He said to love your neighbor, He meant any other person or group, including, but not limited to, the people who live next door.

It is safe, then, to assume Jesus meant to define "neighbor" as any individual or group of individuals who live on the same planet as you do. You *do not* need to:

- Know them

- Agree with them

- Commit to a long-term relationship with them

- Look like them

- Speak the same language as them

- Worship the same way as they do

- Be richer or poorer or just as rich or poor as they are

- Live in the same town, state, country, continent, or hemisphere

- Solve all their problems

- Solve ANY of their problems

- Be successful in helping (Your sincere effort is blessed.)

- Endanger yourself

To love your neighbor as yourself, all you really need to do is whatever you can for whomever you can, whenever you can

As Yourself?
This is Jesus' way of telling us we should love ourselves. God loves us unconditionally. He made us and knows us better than we know ourselves.

If He loves us and we don't love ourselves, then we're far too hard on ourselves. That doesn't mean we shouldn't try to improve and grow, especially in our faith, but God loves you right now as you are.

Even those of us with self-esteem issues still look out for, take care of, and pray (at least a little) for ourselves.

Jesus wants us to do the same for anyone we meet; to look out for, take care of, and pray for our neighbor. He wants us to serve them and help them if they need it. Prayer does both.

Some Ideas to help you pray for people are in **Appendix 3**

10. Praying for People – A Case Study

This is a short story about three young people and the interrelationship of their prayers. Although it is simple at first, the things God does in the lives of these three people are miraculous.

They all love and trust the Lord, and He rewards their faith with amazing life experiences.

This scenario is between Leo, Chad, and Barbara:

Background

- Leo is friends with Chad, but not as close as when they were younger.

- Leo is in (unrequited) love with Barbara and has been since he was seven.

- Chad is dating Barbara.

- As Christians and members of Barbara's father's church, all three pray daily.

- Leo prays for Chad, who is struggling with his college decision.

- Chad, under a lot of stress, prays for himself and guidance.

- Barbara prays too, but for her future ministry, for which she is all-in.

Leo's Prayer

Leo is a bright, reasonably presentable B student attending public school at Arlington High School in his hometown, the Chicago suburb of Arlington Heights, Illinois. He went to grade school with his friend Chad before Chad headed off to private school.

Although he is a decent student, he is not consistently on the honor roll due to occasional struggles in math. Leo will graduate in the spring and plans to go to the University of Illinois at Chicago, so he can commute into the city and live at home.

He has no idea what he wants to do with his life but plans to major in business, as does his twin sister Cleo who plans to do it at Robert Morris University.

Leo is obsessed with two things — figuring out how to get Barbara to notice him, and in a related matter, wishing and hoping Chad would go to Stanford and not Northwestern. (He could also go to Madagascar or Borneo or anywhere, as long as it's far away from Barbara.)

If Chad goes to Northwestern, Leo's chances with Barbara won't be good because Chad would still be close by. He decides to pray for Chad to go to Stanford, which, he convinces himself, is the best place for Chad. He prays like this:

> *Dear God,*
>
> *Thank You for this beautiful day and all the good things You pour into my life. I am grateful for Your persistent power and patience with me, a sinner who is trying to get better.*

Lord, as You know, I am madly in love with Barbara. Unfortunately, she doesn't really know I'm alive. Well, she does, but she is not interested in me in a romantic way. You know?

She's in love with Chad, my friend from elementary school. He is smarter, better looking, with more talents than I ever dreamed of.

Lord, Chad has narrowed his college choices to Stanford and Northwestern. I think Stanford would be much better for him. He would be closer to the wine country. He would be warm and comfortable every day. And his chances of being President one day are much better at Stanford than at Northwestern. I also think the debate team is better there, but don't quote me on that.

Anyway, Lord, I just wanted to pray, you know, for Chad, as he makes his choice. Thank You for helping him make the right choice to go to Stanford.

In Jesus' name, AMEN!

He neglects to mention to God that this decision might enable him to get closer to Barbara so he can go out with her, given her boyfriend would be so far away.

Realizing it in prayer, Leo tried to assure God he is pulling for Stanford *only* because he believes it is *best for Chad.* Chad's relationship with Barbara would be collateral damage, a sacrifice for the larger good. "These things happen all the time," he tells God.

I don't know if God smirks, but if He does, he surely did it listening to Leo try to manipulate Him.

Chad's Prayer

Chad, with whom Leo went to school through fifth grade, attends Northridge Preparatory School in nearby Niles.

Chad looks like a movie star, only taller. As captain of the debate team, president of the National Honor Society, star midfielder on the lacrosse team, and nationally ranked swimmer (4 x 100 individual medley), Chad is a busy guy who makes it look easy.

Chad has narrowed his original list of over three hundred colleges, each offering him full scholarships for either debate, lacrosse, swimming, or all three. He will choose between Northwestern University in nearby Evanston, Illinois, and Stanford University in Palo Alto, California.

Chad is under a lot of stress. His father, the former Governor of Illinois and Undersecretary of Labor, has destined his only son for a career in politics. Chad is ready for his next step, except he is a seventeen-year-old boy who looks at Stanford and Northwestern as radically different places — each with significant risks if he chooses and then realizes he made a mistake. His father is getting impatient for an answer, seeing his indecision as childish.

Chad prays this way:

> *Oh, Lord,*
>
> *Thank You for hearing me and for Your uncanny ability to understand what I'm going through.*

Lord, I am so afraid. Everybody thinks I have this great situation, and I admit it is a nice set of problems to have. But they're still problems, and I know I can miss big-time if I choose wrong.

I ask Your guidance because You know far better than I do, what I'm going to do, where I am going to go, who I am going to meet — all the important things that will happen.

I know I can't know now about all my future (that would probably be terrifying), but I need some help to feel good about my decision.

Lord, direct my steps and help me know in my heart and mind whether it should be Stanford or Northwestern. Here is what I like and don't like about each one...

Chad's prayer continues with a detailed pro and con for both schools. It is a long prayer as he pours out his hopes and fears to God, surrenders to His power and glory, and expectantly waits for the answer.

He thanks God in Jesus' name and goes to sleep. Because of his faith, he sleeps very well.

Barbara's Prayer

Meanwhile, Barbara has been praying too.

Barbara is also a senior at Arlington High. She is the youngest child of Pastor Tommy, the Senior Pastor of a non-denominational Christian church in Arlington Heights. After graduation, she will attend Wheaton College in nearby Wheaton, IL, and live at home.

Barbara plans to enter the ministry upon graduation, as her two brothers and older sister have done. "The family business," as her father calls it.

She plans to marry at some point and have a family — all in their proper season. But in this season, she is focused on her education and the ministry she is called to pursue.

She likes Chad and enjoys spending time with him. But she has no thoughts about a long-term future with him. Their goals in life are too different.

Barbara is a bright, thoughtful young woman. She has been brought up in the church, and though she has some questions, she is all-in for the Lord. She is strong, smart, confident, and independent.

Barbara's prayers all relate to these priorities. She prays like this:

> Lord, Jesus, thank You for hearing my prayers. Thank You for sharing Your wisdom with me, as I am struggling with a decision and need Your guidance.
>
> As you know, my boyfriend Chad and I are moving in vastly different directions in life and our education. I feel as though it would be a good idea for us to go our separate ways now, so we can get fully focused on what is next.
>
> He is a nice guy, but his goals are so different from mine, I can't imagine it working for very long. I'd just prefer to end it now so we can remain friends and hopefully not hurt any feelings.

Lord, You know my passion is to serve You and to be a pastor of whichever people You give me to help. I continue to assure You that I want You to use me to build Your kingdom, whether it is here in Arlington Heights or somewhere else, and to share the gospel with as many people as possible.

Help me to take steps every day toward that goal.

In your name, I pray, AMEN!

How God Might Answer

Factoring in the respective wants and needs of Leo, Chad, and Barbara, God answers their prayers.

Chad's prayer was answered first.

Chad wasn't so much interested in which school he would go to. He trusted the Lord but did not want to override His will. He just wanted to decide confidently and know the decision was approved by God. There *is* one right choice for Chad. At only one of these schools, he will meet his future wife. At only one of these schools, he will earn a Rhodes scholarship.

The next morning, when he opened his eyes, his mind immediately told him where he would go to school. Immediately, he was at peace with the decision and trusts and knew exactly who the answer came from. He is elated.

Barbara received one answer immediately and had to wait a few years for the other.

Barbara is thinking like the mature, intelligent girl she is. Wise beyond her years, she trusts the Lord's perfect timing and His understanding of her wants and needs and the needs of others. Her faith is such that she has total confidence that she will receive what she needs when she needs it.

Barbara knew very quickly it was the right thing to end her relationship with Chad. When she spoke to him, Chad smiled and told her he had been thinking about the same thing. They agreed to stay friends, but from then on went their separate ways.

She knew she would have to wait for her church.

And wait, she did.

Leo Reacts to God's Answers.

He has prayed, expectantly, to God. He has been specific and detailed in his request. He will continue to pray this prayer every day, even after Chad makes his choice (because, either way, he could theoretically change his mind.)

He asks humbly. Not demanding. He follows the rules for prayer, except for trying to fool God by leaving his motives out.

All systems go! Chad should pack his bags! Go west, young man!

Not so fast.

Although God always answers your prayers, you will not always like the answer. God answered Leo's immediate prayer in such a way: *Chad would stay local and attend Northwestern University.* Leo continued to pray for Stanford, but Chad would not change his mind.

But God also heard the rest of Leo's prayer that he loves Barbara and wants to be with her. God read his heart and Barbara's and made plans to answer their other prayers in due time.

God knows Barbara's needs as a woman, daughter, pastor, student, counselor, spiritual advisor to the president, wife, mother, and friend. He will answer her prayers about these needs by giving her exactly what she needs.

God knows about all Chad's needs as a man, son, student, Rhodes Scholar, State Senator, Congressman, Secretary of Commerce, Vice President, and President of the United States. He knows Chad's present, past, and future. He knew Chad was praying for wisdom as he worked to make his decision.

God knows what Leo's needs as a man, son, student, intern, law clerk, junior litigator, lawyer, partner, President of the Illinois Bar Association, mentor, church elder, husband, and friend. God knows who his wife will be. He knows where he will live, how many children they will have, and everything else about his future life.

He also knows what Leo was thinking, and he was not thinking about what is best for Chad. Or Barbara. Or anybody else. Just himself. By directing Chad to Northwestern, against Leo's desire, He took the opportunity to refine in a small way, Leo's immature, selfish streak.

Fast-forward Thirty Years

Leo had a successful legal career, from which he could retire, and he lives in nearby Hoffman Estates, IL. He is close to his boyhood home, so they see his parents regularly. His in-laws are nearby as well.

It is Saturday night, date night. He plans to take his wife out to celebrate their anniversary. In the car, she is half-listening to Leo's thoughts on the next day's activities while reviewing notes on her iPad.

At Luciano's, he looks across the table into the most beautiful brown eyes you have ever seen. He is entranced by her smile. He must look ridiculous because Barbara snaps him out of it.

"Leo! Close your mouth before you drool!" Her laugh is infectious.

"Can't help it. It's you." He replies, resuming his trance.

"Who, me? But why pray, tell?" she responds with mock naiveté.

"Just that you are such a blessing. I love you more every day. And I am so happy I kept on praying, even after Mr. President decided to go to Northwestern. Funny how things work out. I meet you at age seven, fall in love with you immediately, pine for you for nineteen years, finally get to date you, then lose you again when you move to *Borneo*, breaking my heart. Then you came back and were so focused on starting your ministry that I had to start courting you all over again. But now, with all that's happened, and looking at you now, I would do it all again, as many times as I needed to. Prayer is an underrated but highly effective weapon!"

"Well, it works. I prayed for you too. And even though it took ten years and a lot of twists and turns, the Lord came through like He always does."

God has answered Leo's prayer. And Barbara's. And Chad's too. This is a fairy tale ending, of course, but God invented fairy tale endings. (He just calls them endings. Others call them miracles.)

He may take you on a convoluted path. It may involve pain, loss, delay, disappointment, and other forms of struggle.

If you are impatient and cannot or will not wait for God, you can fashion your own solution. You have free will. You do not have to do what God says. Do you think you know better? Have at it!

You may end up happy, fulfilled, and successful, and all other good things.

Or you may not.

In this case, Barbara and Leo had to wait, wonder, and be patient and, at times, be exasperated. But in letting them go through this, God did a few things:

1. Both Barbara and Leo were stubborn and impatient. Like many young people, they wanted it all, and they wanted it quickly. By taking His time, God taught them patience and trust.

2. Through their marriage, He provided a wonderful example of a godly relationship to the community and the church where Barbara is the pastor.

3. In going through some ups and downs, before and during their courtship, they had the time to learn about each other. By the time of their wedding, they were 110 percent certain that they wanted to spend their lives together.

4. By joining these two faithful people, God provided a launching pad for the next generation of Christians.

   a) Leo Jr., their firstborn, entered the ministry after attending his mother's alma mater and eventually took over for his grandfather when he retired from active ministry. He grew to be rather... big. (At 6'8, 290 lbs., no one will call "Junior.") His nickname in college is "The Planet."

   b) Rachel attended Northwestern, where she met and eventually married the president's (aka Chad's) son, Brad. She bakes chocolate chip cookies for the security detail, so her Secret

Service code name is "Cookie." She uses her platform to help bridge the gaps that often exist between Christians, non-believers, and those of different faith traditions.

c) Leah is a starter on the U.S. Women's National Soccer team. She has skillfully parlayed her fame into a job at CNN, where her knowledge of religion, sports, and politics enable her to make a unique contribution in three fields of expertise. In her spare time, she studies for the Illinois bar exam to follow in her father's footsteps.

d) Isaiah worked for the town of Arlington Heights in the IT department. As part of his job, he developed an app for smartphones that is a part social network, part tax and fee payment, part voter registration tool, and part emergency communication channel for his town. After a successful implementation that earned the town and Isaiah personally, great reviews, and a measure of fame, he sold the idea to Cisco for two hundred million dollars. His app is now the standard for the next generation of municipal management and civic engagement tools. His brother calls him, "Isaiah the profit."

e) All four kids remain active in the church and in building the kingdom of the Lord throughout their lives.

Leo, who is now known as "Senior," is a full nine inches shorter and ninety-five pounds lighter than his son, is healthy and content.

Retired from his law firm, he does the legal work for both Barbara's church and Leo Jr.'s, and he served as a church elder and a mentor. He also serves on the boards of directors of several private companies and non-profit philanthropic organizations.

He has shared his faith testimony at several area churches, including Barbara's and his father-in-law's. His message to others is one of patience and persistent prayer. It is moving, funny, and inspiring.

He'll admit his feeble, unsuccessful teenage attempts to manipulate God by suggesting he only wanted 'the boyfriend' to go to Stanford because the weather was better there. He will laugh at himself.

He will refer to his rival for Barbara's affections as "some guy who lives in Washington, you might have heard of him."

It's a great story, and he tells it very well because he enjoys telling it as much or more than his audience enjoys hearing it.

Final Thoughts from Chicagoland

A few comments before we leave our Chicago area friends:

- Patience in prayer and while waiting for an answer is critical, not only to your particular need but for your spiritual growth and maturity.

- Realize that although God answers every prayer, he's not a vending machine, automatically churning out exactly what you ask for. Remember, only Chad and Barbara got most of what they asked for. Leo did not. But God's answer to Leo, though delayed, was better than he could have imagined.

- God has an infinite perspective, so it is likely that given an unlimited view and insight, he will answer your prayer in a different way than you pray it. This also works to address your immediate issue and your long-term spiritual growth.

- This case study is simple, with only three people involved, but you can infer a lot of ripples from these events with just a little imagination:

- Chad becomes President—think of how his candidacy and administration might affect people across the country and around the world.

- In winning the Presidency, the incumbent whom Chad defeated then retired from public life. Large numbers of careers were started, ended, or changed by his election. (This is not unusual but underlines the impact of a change in leadership).

- In her years of ministry, Barbara brought many people to the Lord, bringing meaning, joy, and hope to these new believers. She also married many couples and officiated at many funerals.

- Some of those she ministered to became ministers themselves (who created their own ripples in the process of building the Kingdom).

- Leo loved to mentor young people. He felt like he had made so many mistakes that he could help others avoid those errors. The church, the Bar Association, and his practice provide him with a steady stream of people who are open to and in great need of guidance. Whatever success they have is due in part to Leo's efforts.

- And so on, and so on, and so on…

- All these results and millions more were put in motion by the singular prayers of three people. From those three requests, offered in faith and hope, with humility and expectation, God made all these results.

- Chad, Barbara, and Leo are good people and are loved by God. **You are too**!

- And because God loves you so much, He wants to answer your prayers and bless your life the way He did for them.

- Because of God's infinite capacity, he cares about and answers all sincere prayers and requests. None are more important than any other. If you care about it and pray honestly and patiently as Jesus directed, He will answer you.

Some Ideas to help you pray for people are in **Appendix 3**

11. Praying for People: Do My Prayers Matter?

God's Priority Is People in Need

When we pray for people — ourselves or someone else — we are praying about God's priority. Because He loves us more than we could ever imagine, the prayer for another person or group of people is the one He hears first and with the greatest urgency. He loves everyone involved in your prayer. That includes the person doing the praying (you) and the person or people you're praying for. Although God doesn't need a to-do list, if He had one, people in need would be at the top.

But there are needs, and there are NEEDS, right? I need my coffee in the morning, or I can only be expected to function at 70 percent of capacity (and that's generous).

But I NEED people who care about me, my health, a job, a place to live, freedom from tyranny, reasonable safety, and security, and so on.

If I am in the way of a hurricane, I NEED shelter in a safe place for my family and me, high enough not to be swept away by floodwaters.

I need a break after a long meeting to go outside and get some air.

Even though I have a car, I need a new one.

But if I have no car, I have no way to get to work, so I NEED a car that runs, new or otherwise.

Which is more important, NEED, or need? Well, one may be more urgent, more serious, more acceptable to pray for. The other may be one of those times when you feel a little selfish **(see in Chapter 3, here)**.

How does God view it? They are the same. What His children need or NEED are both important to Him. He answers these prayers with equal priority.

> *Wait a minute, if my home is about to be demolished by a tsunami, and my cousin is lonesome and wants to play 'Dungeons and Dragons,' and we both pray, God handles both prayers the same? That's nuts!*

If you were a dispatcher for a police department, ambulance, or fire department, then yes, handling those two calls with equal priority is nuts. They would come to get you to safety one hundred times out of one hundred. Or they would try to.

The kid with the Dungeons and Dragons request, well, he may have to wait. (Unless they arrest him for calling 911 to play a game.)

Because these departments have limited resources, including people, equipment, and most of all TIME, they must prioritize.

God is not limited by resources, including time, which His power transcends. God can, if He so chooses, deliver you from the tsunami or even calm the waters and leave everyone wondering what happened to it.

At the same time, he can scare up some friends for your cousin to play his game with, again, if he so chooses. He can make sure your cousin's need for friends and a game, even as he is dealing with your life and death NEED facing a tsunami.

For some matters, which God knows will occur, He provides, in advance, His solution. One of humanity's oldest and most ubiquitous inventions is the shoelace.

Small children, adults, hockey players, FBI agents, priests, bus drivers, game show hosts, nurses, and loggers all seem to have nothing in common, but they do. They all must tie their shoes. If they don't, their shoes fall off. And we don't want that. We need them to stay on. In fact, if you are at the North Pole, you NEED your shoes to stay on, or you might lose your foot to frostbite.

We don't normally pray for tying our shoes. Why would we when we have real NEEDS and even some other needs? Why waste precious one-on-one time with God talking about tying my shoes?

You wouldn't. And you wouldn't need to. God has already anticipated your need for secure shoes. But you do need to trust Him, with all needs, all NEEDS, and even many wants, because He has already arranged for their provision.

The Complexity of Tying Your Shoes

Yes, you say, but tying my shoes is simple. I don't really need God to help with it.

Are you sure? Think about the various things that need to be in place for you to tie your shoe. If I'm walking to the office, and my shoe becomes untied, I need to be able to:

- See my shoe

- Feel my feet

- Notice my shoe getting looser

- Hear the laces flopping about

- Walk

- Stop

- Stoop down

- Manipulate the laces

- Make the "bunny ears" (you know — the loops you use to make the knot)

- Pull the ears tight

- Stand back up again

- Go on with my day

Not to mention the other things God gave or did for me to assist in resolving my "simple" problem:

- A parent or teacher who taught me to tie my shoes fifty-six years ago

- A brain to retain and repeat the process daily for most of my life

- Spatial awareness so that I didn't trip anyone, and no one fell over me

- Safety and protection so that I didn't get kicked or yelled at for being stooped down on a busy sidewalk

- Awareness of surroundings so that, among other managed risks, no cars, bikes, or scooters ran over me

- I didn't lose the important papers I had with me

- It didn't start to rain, snow, or hail

- No volcanoes erupted (nearby, at least)

- There were few, if any, locusts, frogs, velociraptors, or gnats, and if there were any, they weren't there to attack me

You get the idea. When you think about a "simple" problem like tying your shoelace, you're not suffering much angst about how you will solve it.

You don't think of it like this, but you depended on God anyway. Without His grace, love, and mercy, not to mention the power to adjust your surroundings, provide you with education, and a cute analogy like "bunny ears," you might not even have shoes.

You might not even have feet!

Pray to the Lord *First*

How much more, then, do we depend on Him when the problems are complex, illogical, chronic, recurrent, contentious, fluid, and/or highly emotional?

When you can't sort out all the factors, or even all the people involved, the timeline, or the alternative responses, you need help. The first place to look is to God. Why?

Because God sees the whole playing field, including:

- Opportunities and risks.

- Resources — human, natural, financial, or physical — that you either can't see or aren't noticing.

- The needs of everyone involved.

- The future and the past for everyone involved.

Praying to the Lord FIRST can unlock all the other things you need to solve the problem. He will put those things at your disposal in His perfect timing, synchronize their actions and reactions, and solve the problem His way, which is, by definition, perfect.

When we say *perfect*, do we mean "easy, fun, or comfortable, without negative consequences?" Not necessarily. God's ways are perfect because His knowledge of us, His goals for us, and His awareness of the circumstances surrounding us at all times, in real-time, enable Him to take just the right actions at just the right time, every time.

Alas, perfect does not equate to ease, fun, comfort, etc. It doesn't mean we will enjoy the solution. We may, but God is more interested in our growth than our comfort or enjoyment. Perfect solutions add to our incremental, consistent growth of faith, love, and trust, as managed by God.

Further, the Lord knows the full extent of your journey and always has. He knows where you came from, where you are, and where you are going. Your spiritual growth is in His perfect hands.

> "...Truly I tell you, if you have faith as small as a mustard seed, you can say to this mountain, 'Move from here to there,' and it will move. Nothing will be impossible for you."
>
> Matthew 17:20 NIV

Some Ideas to help you pray for people are in **Appendix 3**

For some insight on why your prayers matter, see **Appendix 9**

Part 4
Praying for Things

12.   What Is a Thing?

Broadly Defined

Because I didn't want to write (and you surely didn't want to read), a book with twenty-nine thousand chapters detailing every different "thing," I grouped them under the amorphous heading of "things." A thing can be:

- A physical object

- A situation like a job, a romantic relationship, a spot on a team, or being cast as Snow White in the spring play

- A hope like you hope your child gets into college or the Red Sox win the World Series

- A way of life, such as living in New York City, working on Wall Street, and living in a high-rise condo building or going completely off the grid in northwestern Montana

- An idea, like crowdsourcing, hydroponic farms, Medicare for all, or even Christianity

- Wisdom, which is unique and thus has its own chapter, but is still essentially a "thing" (see Chapter 13)

There is an infinite variety of things under the heading of "things." This section deals with how to pray for them. Suffice to say, if what you want is neither human nor wisdom, then it is a "thing."

The alternative, if we didn't lump them together, we would have a chapter, each, on:

- socks
- shovels
- chimichangas
- world peace
- weight loss
- rabbits
- quiet
- money
- Southern Connecticut State University
- Bouffant hairstyles
- Vail, Colorado
- Charlize Theron
- the B-52s
- oatmeal
- pine trees
- Hyundai
- stone walls

- "Big Little Lies"

- rain

- snow

- sleet

- ice cube trays…

- …And every other "thing!"

You get the idea. Laborious, unhelpful, and unnecessary.

So, just think of whatever "thing" you want to pray for as you read my thoughts on praying for "things."

Can We Ask Him for Anything?

God answers every prayer. To our impatient human minds, this seems untrue; we want what we want, right now. We don't like to wait, especially when our perceived need is urgent. His answer always includes His perfect:

- Insight into the request and what is driving it

- Timing

- A solution to your problem

- Determination of what we need

Sometimes our sense of want and God's assessment of our needs are in sync. Then we get both what we want and need. Other times, God does not deliver what you want for a wide variety of reasons, including:

- What you want is not His will (e.g., you want a gun so that you can shoot someone you don't like.).

- You are asking for a selfish reason (e.g., you want a new car, not because you need one, but because your neighbor is the envious type and you like to make them miserable).

- God has something better in mind for what you need (e.g., He allows a political candidate to lose an election for the Senate but allows them to become CEO of a large company where he can do more good and be more content.).

- God's timing and your sense of urgency are different (e.g., You want to play the lead in the school play this year, but God's plan calls for you to play the lead next year).

God hears every prayer we pray. He does not care what language you speak, race, ethnicity, or even religious organization you belong to or don't belong to. Our relationship is with Him, not a church building, a skin color, a home country, or religious denomination. He loves us and wants to be with us forever in heaven. God does not create barriers between Himself and us. And we shouldn't either.

Given His eternal perspective, God does not answer prayers as though there was a rush. He can perfectly solve everything, for everyone, everywhere, with a snap of His fingers, but that is not how He works.

God knows what we need now, what we needed yesterday, and what we will need fifteen and even fifty years from now.

Whatever the underlying issue, God is already working on it. A lot of underlying issues never surface. God fixes them before you even know they are there.

How God Might Answer – Praying for Things

We have mentioned God will answer your prayer, and He may do so differently than you had asked. So, because it's not your way, you might be tempted to consider the prayer unanswered. God doesn't have to act with blazing speed to your requests. He can but often doesn't because there is more to it.

For one thing, there's the matter of need and want. God is not a vending machine or Amazon.com. Those services assume you know what you need/want, and they deliver it. Period.

Amazon doesn't make the distinction because the customer knows what they ordered, whether a true need or a want. Amazon doesn't care which. They have no interest in preparing you for eternity. They just need the card transaction to go through.

God's process is not simply, "see-the-order, fill-the-order." He investigates your request. He discerns what your motivation is for making the request. He knows if you are asking for something with sincere purposes in mind. He knows if you're praying for the right thing for the wrong reasons.

Then God looks at what you need. It isn't that God is against a want. He will answer prayers for things you simply want. But His priority is always what you need. If your wants conflict with your needs, your needs win every time.

So, You Want a Lamborghini?

An example might be that you want a Lamborghini Aventador. (It's a car. A pretty nice one.)

You don't have the needed $460,000 (base, not fully loaded, I'm guessing) to buy one. So you pray for it.

God hears your prayers for the Aventador. He considers motives and finds you simply want one. There is nothing sinister or unsavory. You're one step closer to your dream car!

God doesn't consider the price. It's meaningless to Him in the equation. If He decides to let you get a Lamborghini, a large part of that is paying for it. Nice! Another step closer!

But not so fast. He will also look at your need:

- You need to have reliable transportation to get back and forth from your summer job scooping ice cream and running bumper boats and mini-golf on Cape Cod.

- You need a vehicle that will transport your mini-fridge, your Xbox 360, your shoes, and all your clothes back to college.

- You need to save as much money as you can to minimize what will otherwise be crippling college debt. (You are paying for the car—you didn't ask God for a winning lottery ticket! If you did, He would consider the same factors.)

God's determination: you *need* a vehicle, but you *DO NOT need* a $460,000 car that goes two hundred miles per hour.

In fact, not only do you not need one, God knows you would find you don't really want one either.

Imagine parking a car like that overnight in a college town. You would never be able to sleep worrying about vandalism, theft, and zany college hijinks.

God's Answer: Need Defeats Want

Through a series of overt and subliminal means, God persuades you that what you REALLY want (that is, what you actually NEED) is a used, 17-year-old Toyota Camry.

The car, which a little old lady who only drove back and forth to the grocery store and to church just traded to the dealer, is sixteen years old and has been driven only nine thousand miles. And, it's Midnight Blue.

(The little old lady may have traded the Camry for a Lamborghini, but for this example, it doesn't matter.)

Unlike the Lamborghini, the Camry checks all your "NEED" boxes.

- It costs only $5,699, which you can handle with a loan.

- It has new tires.

- The inside is clean and like new.

- It is the perfect solution to what you (and God) know you need.

So, you get the Camry. It works out great. You end up taking care of the car and drive it over two hundred thousand miles, and you sell it when you and your spouse have your third child.

And when you sell, the buyer is another college kid.

Did God answer your prayer?

13. Praying for Things: Do My Prayers Matter?

Selfish or Entitled? Asking with Expectations

"Therefore I tell you, whatever you ask in prayer, believe that you have received it, and it will be yours."
Mark 11:24 ESV

Jesus tells us to pray expectantly. Pray as though you already have it, and you will have it. There is a lot to this seemingly simple verse, but for our purposes, it is a command of the Lord and a reassurance you will have what you pray for.

We interpret expectation in several ways, based on our limited understanding of the "ask, wait, get-or-don't get, ask-again-or-whine" cycle that we engage in human life. We might think someone praying for a thing this way is:

- **Unduly entitled**, suggesting they deserve something simply because they asked.

- **Tragically disorganized**, praying for something they may already have, just in case.

- **Naive** or **Lazy**, who has given up making any "real" effort and has substituted the mysticism of prayer for doing any "real" work.

People may think this way, but God doesn't. He has directed us to pray with expectation. He won't think less of us when we obey this direction.

So we're not lazy, spoiled, disorganized, or naive.

We are, instead, obedient, faithful, and trusting of the Lord.

God can do things that are impossible for human beings to do. He has control over all things, everywhere. He is not constrained by time or space. He can act on all of creation or just a hair on your head, with perfect precision, timing, and execution.

His answer could go in an unexpected direction, and depending on what it is or your reasons for asking for it, He may choose not to precisely deliver your "order."

But we also take it on faith that He loves us and knows what is best in all situations. His answers to our prayers are always right and always for our best, ultimate good. Our prayer may be flawed, but His answer is always perfect.

What's Really Happening?

When we pray for a thing—an object, opportunity, or something else—that is just for us, with no other intention but to gratify ourselves, we can feel selfish or spoiled when we get what we prayed for.

God won't spoil you.

Unlike some human fathers, who may overindulge their children as a substitute for a deeper relationship with them, God knows us better than we know ourselves. He knows our past, present, and future. He knows His plans for us.

Part of His plan is the continual refinement that He patiently works on for those who have accepted His gift of salvation. Refinement is the systematic removal of faults and impurities. It is a critical process for any artisan as they do their work. The result is a purer, more precious commodity, one more valuable than in its unrefined state.

God is an expert craftsman, whose handiwork includes all of creation, including all people. But we arrive on earth as flawed projects because of the sin in the world. We are all broken in many ways due to the evil in the world.

God sees us as unfinished works of fine art. He continually works on each of us, day, and night, throughout our lives. He teaches us to live in harmony with Him, through His Word, and through the examples of others in our daily lives.

Although we have free will and can choose not to follow God's directives, we are not immune to the consequences. Negative outcomes are associated with rebelling against God. This doesn't mean He no longer loves you. Quite the opposite! He does not abandon you because you are His beloved child.

He does not give up on you because you made a mistake — or a million mistakes. But He will correct you with consequences for your actions. He wants you to learn and understand His way is best. Whether or not we can see it, His way is always better than our way.

Praying expectantly is what Jesus tells us to do. So it cannot, by definition, be spoiled, selfish, pointless, or naive.

Is It Selfish to Pray for Things?

When we pray for things, we have a purpose for those things. Maybe they are a gift for someone, maybe they are for ourselves. Maybe they are strictly optional, amusement objects or situations. Or they may involve crucial survival needs like water and food.

Selfishness, or caring only about oneself, can be identified in the motives of the one seeking the thing.

Here are two simple examples, one with, No (not selfish) and Yes (selfish):

No (Not Selfish)

The year was 1945, and Mary Lou was graduating from high school outside of Baltimore. Maryland.

More than anything else, she wanted to be a nurse. She was smart, strong, unfailingly kind, and serious without being stern. Her smile lit up the countryside.

The problem was getting the money together for nursing school, for which her father refused to pay. Mom prayed and prayed. She asked God for His help. There were no school loans back then. She had no wealthy benefactors whom she felt like she could approach.

She prayed daily, sometimes hourly, because she wanted it more than anything.

Finally, after several months, and after the program she had wanted to join had started, her father came to her, clearly looking for a way to help.

They talked, and he seemed adamant it was a bad idea for him to pay for her schooling. But he could see how much she wanted this. It wasn't a little kid wanting a pony. This was a young woman who wanted to make a difference. After many tears and many words, some of them heated, he finally agreed to pay for her schooling.

BUT, this gift would be all her future birthday presents, her wedding present, and all the gifts she might get for as long as he lived. He may have gone on for some time listing the future gifts she was receiving now, but she didn't hear him. She was too busy hugging him.

Granddad was trying to hold the line on spending. He also didn't think women needed education. But he could also see how his daughter wanted to do great things, how excited she was to help others, and he couldn't say no. Granddad gave in because God softened his heart and, in so doing, answered Mom's prayers.

Yes (Selfish)

The second example is from when I was ten years old. My friends, the DeVincentis brothers, had all gotten orange Chopper bicycles for Christmas. They were so cool and seemed so fast. I was as jealous as I've ever been about anything.

Although I didn't know what I was doing, I tried to pray like I saw kids do in movies sometimes. It wasn't the Lord's Prayer, the cornerstone of our nightly prayers. (In Eastern Massachusetts, we called it the *"Aahh Faaaahthah"* or "Our Father" if you don't speak Boston.)

No, there was no rote memorization in this prayer. I poured my heart out to God. The only problem was that I didn't pray for a Chopper. I prayed for a bike faster than the Chopper. I forgot to ask for it to be a cooler one too.

I didn't pray for it every day, but when I did, it was usually in response to getting left in the dust by the DeVincentis brothers and their wicked cool bikes.

The next Christmas, my prayer was answered.

Sort of.

When my brother and I got up Christmas morning, two bikes were parked in front of the tree in the living room. They were identical as our gifts tended to be since there were only eleven months separating us.

Nonetheless, I am sure my face registered disappointment, although maybe my parents missed it. The bikes were not Choppers or Sting Rays. They didn't look like the kind of bike you put baseball cards on the spokes, secured with clothespins.

Everyone called this kind of bike, an English bike. They were black, had regular handlebars, and large narrow tires. It also had three speeds, which was more than the Choppers of my friends. Still, it was not cool looking. At all.

It was the kind of bike Mary Poppins would ride or Miss Gulch in the *Wizard of Oz*.

Given that there were ten inches of snow outside that Christmas, I didn't need to fake my enthusiasm and run out to ride it. Mom wouldn't have let me since I was in my robe and pajamas. So I thought about it and when the nice weather came, and the bikes came out, I had my tall, black, not at all cool, bike.

The Chopper boys laughed until we started having races. I learned bigger tires could help you go faster — MUCH faster than a Chopper and faster than every other bike in the neighborhood.

My prayer was selfish because it was driven only by my desire to be 'better than' my friends. (*Don't judge me, I was ten!*)

But God knew what I needed and what I wanted. He knew what was driving this, as He had okayed the Choppers the previous year.

The need was no problem, but the want was for the wrong reason. To be better than another kid because of a bike was not the right motive, and God wanted me to understand that. So he answered my prayer with my need, but not my want — a faster bike, but not a not at all cool one.

But then I guess maybe He felt a little bit bad, so He made my Mary Poppins bike much faster than everyone else's.

God certainly considers your motives in deciding when and how to answer your prayers. When you pray for things, God's consideration is for the thing second, but the person and their growth, first.

In the case of my mother, God had long planned for her to take care of the sick. Her natural empathy, sense of humor, and selfless, hard-working attitude were gifts He had already given her in preparation for the important work she did.

In making her wait a bit, He asked her to trust Him. And she did. So He didn't make her wait long before going to work on her Dad, who relented and enabled her dream to get started.

In my case, being younger and dumber, His lesson for me was more straightforward. Don't be jealous of others. They have what they have; you have what you have. Be satisfied. Be grateful. Envy and jealousy are lies that Satan tells you to make you feel bad about yourself.

I wish I could say I found Jesus and followed Him from that day. But I took a lot longer to figure anything out. But He waited and kept doing things for me.

Even now, as I am typing this story about the bike, I am realizing another time when God was working on me, refining and teaching me and my character and getting me ready for whatever was next.

It's really cool when He does that.

So, in summary, ask for things — bikes, football helmets, goalie pads, the girl you want to take to the prom, the woman you want to marry, the place you want to go on vacation, the job you want that will make you rich (or happy), etc. Ask for them.

Ask for them in faith, trust, and love. Ask for them with expectation. Ask for them for the right reasons. If possible, plan to share the thing when you get it.

Ask for the thing for a positive, helpful reason. You are allowed to enjoy yourself. Just don't hurt anyone else in any way.

You are a child of God. People watch you. Some want to learn from you. Some want you to fail. But you are an example of a believer in Jesus Christ, the Son of the living God. Be a good example.

For ideas for composing prayers for things, see **Appendix 4**

14. Some "Things" Are Special

When it comes to 'things' as we said earlier, there is a broad range. Pretty much anything you might pray for outside of a person is a thing.

So does God think about all 'things' the same way? Yes, and no. God brings you whatever you need for your particular life, mission, interests, and desires. Not necessarily what you want in all cases, but what you need.

The exception has to do with things God specifically lays out as special and for which He makes no distinction as to who needs them. Everybody needs these things, and when we pray for them, we get them, with no questions asked. God is delighted to share these gifts with His people.

These special things are salvation, forgiveness of sins, wisdom, and spiritual growth.

Praying for Salvation

What Is Salvation?
At some point in most people's lives, they consider their own mortality. Maybe it's a health scare, or the birth of a child, or the loss of a parent or a friend.

We start to think about our lives and how they might end. Some consider what comes after our lives on earth end, but not everyone does. They should.

When they do this research, it is sobering. Without God, we are literally doomed — damned — to live in hell for eternity.

The reason we pray for salvation — being rescued from eternity in hell — is because of the difference it makes. Heaven is a truly blissful place, close to God and free of all pain, worry, sorry, or regret. Heaven is paradise. I am grossly understating the pure, endless joy of heaven.

See **Appendix 5** for Ideas about praying for Salvation

Salvation from What?

By contrast, hell is eternal separation from God, with eternal punishment, pain, anguish, and regret. Imagine your very worst day on earth, multiply the severity by a big number, then imagine every day and night for the rest of time is like that. I am grossly understating the endless horror, pain, and anguish of hell.

You hear people joke about hell. They say things like, "I'm going to hell since all my friends will be there." Or, "Oh, gee, I said something bad behind someone's back, I'm going to hell."

A joke is a joke, but if you really think about hell, where there is no hope, no joy, no light, or no love — ever — it's not very funny. In fact, it's the worst possible outcome you could have for your life.

Salvation *Is* Available!

As terrifying as the prospect of hell is, we have a Savior in Jesus Christ. Jesus went to hell to pay for our sins. There he defeated death and rose from the dead three days later. In so doing, Jesus took our punishment on Himself to pay for our sins. As the only perfect person ever to walk the earth, Jesus taking the punishment was a gift of pure love toward all people, even those who were not yet born.

Because Jesus is God, and because God loves all people, he offers this gift to all people. Salvation, the forgiveness of sins, and the home in heaven when your earthly life is over. This is the finest gift you will ever receive. And all you must do is accept it.

There Is No Catch

In our earthly lives, we become conditioned to finding good things and cynically asking, what's the catch? This is because in life on earth, very often, if something seems too good to be true, you'll probably be sorry you didn't just keep walking.

Salvation through Jesus Christ is different — radically, diametrically different.

To obtain salvation, all you need to do is make a heartfelt prayer to God. Thanking Him for his offer of salvation, thanking Him for the sacrifice of His only begotten Son, whom He loved so much.

Then pray about the commitment you are making to let Jesus into all areas and aspects of your life so He can help you in all aspects of your life.

See **Appendix 5** for Ideas about praying for Salvation.

The other good news is that since you did not earn your salvation — Jesus offered it to you by grace — you cannot lose it by failing. Once you have accepted Jesus, He is with you forever.

And as happy as that makes you, it makes Him even happier. Remember what He went through to secure your freedom. How he suffered a heinous, humiliating death. Imagine the amount of sin he took on! Imagine the shame!

That was the price He paid for your salvation. So is He happy when you accept it? Yes, He is.

This Gift Is Irrevocable
It bears repeating. Having accepted this gift from Jesus, you have salvation. It cannot be taken away from you.

Does that mean you can sin indiscriminately and have a "Get out of Jail Free" card whenever you need it? No.

When you accept Jesus, you accept living your life as much like He lived His as possible. Loving and serving others, promoting peace and unity, and in so doing, draw closer to God by being more like Him. You will never be God, but you will become more and more like the risen Jesus.

Key Questions about Salvation

What if God Says No, I'm not Welcome?

He won't if your acceptance is authentic.

God created you just as He did everyone else. Why did He create us? To love us. Since love is not coerced or mandated, God gave us free will to, among many other things, choose whether to accept His gift of salvation.

Once offered, He will not take it back. All who accept His Son, Jesus Christ, are in. There is no exception list.

What if I Don't Accept Salvation?

As noted above, the gift of salvation must be accepted by the person to whom it's offered to save them. And just as loving God is a choice each person is free to make, accepting His eternal gift of salvation is a choice each person needs to make as well.

If you choose not to accept the Lord's salvation, you are essentially saying that you don't need God. That you are comfortable that whatever comes after this life on earth is acceptable to you. You are saying that whatever hell offers up, you're okay with it.

Does God Forget About You If You Refuse His Salvation?

Good question.

No, God never forgets about nor gives up on you, even when you shun Him. A father doesn't stop caring about his child when the child rebels or refuses his support. And God is the perfect Father, so He doesn't stop caring about us.

He continues to love you, care about you, and provide for you all the while, hoping you will change your mind about His salvation.

What If I Refuse His Salvation, But Change My Mind Later?

Unlike God's offer of salvation, which is never taken back, your refusal can always be changed to an acceptance.

One reason God doesn't give up on you when you refuse is you may change your mind. God knows the plan for you, and He can adjust it based on your acceptance of His Son or not.

But He wants very much for you to accept, and if you change your mind, He will be overjoyed. He will provide for you all the same gifts that everyone else who accepts Him can get.

Salvation Is the Start

Having accepted your salvation and committed to loving God and following Jesus, your faith journey is just beginning. But knowing that you have been saved can provide you hope and strength for that journey.

Salvation is just a prayer away.

See **Appendix 5** for Ideas about praying for Salvation

Praying for Forgiveness

Forgiveness is the critical piece of salvation. Without it is to be condemned for your sins, and that would leave salvation as a much hollower gift.

Instead, forgiveness of sins is the star of the show!

What Makes Us Think God Will Forgive Us?

God gave His only begotten Son as a sacrifice for the sins of all people.

Obediently, Jesus gave Himself in sacrifice for those sins. He was sinless in all ways, yet onto his perfect self were loaded all the vileness and evil of humanity. He paid for it all.

He could have disobeyed and performed some miracle to escape or kill all His persecutors or simply force all involved to change their minds and let Him go free. That was not the plan, though. He came into the world to save sinners, of which we all are. Without His sacrifice, we would die. No heaven, not eternal life.

So having made this sacrifice obeying the Father and accepting our punishment, we don't think God will forgive us. We know He will. But in case we were still unsure, the Bible gives us a few assurances, including:

> Let us then approach God's throne of grace with confidence, so that we may receive mercy and find grace to help us in our time of need.
> Hebrews 4:16 NIV

> You, Lord, are forgiving and good, abounding in love to all who call to you.
> Psalm 86:5 NIV

> The LORD is good to all; he has compassion on all he has made.
> Psalm 145:9 NIV

What Does God Expect from Us, in Terms of Mercy?

God wants us to have mercy on each other, just as He has mercy on us. As Jesus told His disciples:

> *"But love your enemies, do good to them, and lend to them without expecting to get anything back. Then your reward will be great, and you will be children of the Most High, because he is kind to the ungrateful and wicked.*
> *Be merciful, just as your Father is merciful."*
> *Luke 6:35–36 NIV*

What Is Sin?

Failing to Obey God – A Short History

God made the world, but He didn't include sin.

In Genesis, describing how He created the world, there was the line, "And in the mid-afternoon of the fourth day, God thought he would shake things up, so He added sin. And He saw that it was bad. Really bad."

It's not there because it didn't happen.

Satan introduced sin to God's perfect world when he tempted Eve to eat from the Tree of Life, the one thing God forbade them from eating in the sumptuous garden.

Then Eve convinced Adam to have some as well, and they immediately knew what guilt was like.

They hid from God, who knew what had happened, just as He knew everything else.

From this original sin, all other evil, corruption, malice, abuse, neglect, hatred, jealousy, and every other sinful act and feeling came into the world.

Later, as God had chosen the nation of Israel and placed for its leader Moses, He saw the people were "rebellious" and "stiff-necked" or stubborn and prone to sin. So the Lord gave Moses the law, which included the famous Ten Commandments.

By obeying the law of Moses, the Israelites could avoid sin. Being human beings with free will, their obedience to the law fluctuated over the years. Through the prophets, God would send warnings that they were sinning, and His judgment and punishment would be severe if they didn't straighten up.

Ultimately, God administered His punishment, and the people cried for mercy. And God would give it. And the cycle would begin again.

When Jesus was asked one day by a Pharisee trying to trap Him on his knowledge of the law, what the most important of the commandments was, Jesus answered in an unexpected way. Instead of choosing one of the ten, he added two more. Known as 'The Great Commission' these two commands, when properly followed, would cover all ten of those given by God to Moses. Here are the verses from the Gospel According to Mark:

> Jesus replied: "'Love the Lord your God with all your heart and with all your soul and with all your mind. This is the first and greatest commandment. And the second is like it: 'Love

your neighbor as yourself.' All the Law and the
Prophets hang on these two commandments."
Matthew 22:37–40 NIV

Forgetting He Is Always with You

God is with you always. No matter where you are or what you are doing, He sees. One risk of falling into sin is falling into the culture around you.

We live in a broken world. God knows that. But He wants you to overcome the world, and He gives you guidance as to how. You must follow that guidance and refrain from sin even if your environment, culture, surroundings, friends, and everything else is sinful or tempting to sin.

He wants to help you avoid these risks, but you must obey. Too often, we don't. Maybe if we remember He is there, we might be more disciplined. Maybe sometimes, but not always.

Sin Is Sin

People try to create a hierarchy of sin. The inference is some sins are more serious than others. And in the world, that is true.

In most places in the world, murder is a serious crime. It is punishable by anything from a long-term in jail to death.

In some countries, theft is as serious as murder. Some penalties include removing the thief's hand as punishment. The item stolen isn't relevant.

We know there is a whole range of sins, including things that are okay in moderation but sinful in excess. There are other things that are sinful whenever they are done. We're not going to list all the sins because that would make for a long, mostly boring book.

The point is, while people look at sins on a range from "not so bad" to "deserving of death," God doesn't.

God hates all sin. It is not from Him; He does not condone one bit of it. It is from Satan, who is the originator and author of all sin, lies, and temptation.

It's important to realize God hates SIN, that is the act itself and the effect it has on ourselves or someone else. However, to conclude He hates SINNERS is wrong, misguided, and misrepresents who God is.

God is love. He created each of us to love us. He does not like everything we do. In fact, He hates our *sins*. But He loves *us*. We are made in His image, and our purpose is to love God and be loved by Him.

So what does God do? He does what the perfect Father would do. His children misbehave, and He corrects them. This may happen partly through earthly consequences, of which there can be many. It may not happen on earth at all. But we know God judges us all, even though we have accepted salvation. We don't lose heaven, but we do have to answer for our sins.

The good news is that God will forgive you if you own and repent of the sin. Just as you accepted salvation with a heartfelt prayer, you can be forgiven of your sins in the same way.

What Sins Does God Never Forgive?

Another common question, but the answer may surprise you.

There is no sin God will not forgive.

As discussed above, for God, sin is sin, so if He can forgive you for one, He would forgive you for all.

BUT, the key here is not the sin, which can be anything, but what matters is the condition of your mind, heart, and soul.

- You must regret the sin.

- You must recognize it as sin.

- You must be remorseful and regretful for the sin.

- You must commit to working to eliminate the recurrence of the sin. This includes asking God for His help.

- Your sole motive is to ask for God's forgiveness.

Always keep in mind God knows all you have done. There is nothing secret from Him. Your relationship with God is based on *your* total transparency, and that is non-negotiable since we are all transparent to God.

But given that transparency, why not simply level with Him? Acknowledge the truth as you know it, give a clear, heartfelt expression of your regret and remorse, and do what you can to avoid doing it again.

Does that mean that you'll never sin again? Probably not. We all struggle with our sinful, human nature. God doesn't expect us to be perfect. But when you do sin, He wants you to own your mistake, admit it, being truly sorry for it, and committing to an effort to never doing the sin again. This is called repentance.

And related to that, if you do it again, and you confess to Him in the same way, He will forgive you again. That is not a "Get out of Jail Free" card. It's better. It's God's mercy and grace, saving you from yourself.

Confessing Your Sins and Mistakes

Regardless of how elaborate the process, and no matter how many other people are involved, your confession of sin, like every other prayer, is between you and God.

God is offended by our sins, and the formal Act of Contrition acknowledges that fact. You should absolutely apologize and repent when you offend God.

You should still apologize and do what you can to make amends when your sin hurts someone else. And God blesses sincere apologies and acting to make the problem better. He is with you when you commit the sin, and He is with you when you own up to it. These are what "good Acts of Contrition" and Penance are — apologies and doing what you can to make it right.

As was the case with your declaration of faith, you can confess your sins any way you want:

- You can pray out loud or to yourself or in writing or in meditation or music or any other medium you wish, in privacy, if that makes you more comfortable.

- You have the option to speak with a priest, rabbi, or pastor if you would like advice and counsel. This is not required by God. Sometimes it is helpful to receive spiritual advice from a leader in the church.

- For the crucial act of confessing the sin itself, you need only tell it to God.

- You could speak to the person you sinned against if there was someone. This provides a head start on penance, or doing what you can to help improve the situation.

The thing is, God already knows what you did, what you neglected to do, or intended to do, regardless of the outcome. So why confess?

We confess to Him for the same reason we give Him thanks and praise, or we ask Him for wisdom or some other thing. You love, respect, and trust Him. He loves you, regardless of your sins. No sin will cause Him to turn His back on you. But he wants your contrition, whether in a formal prayer or heartfelt sorrow expressed some other way.

God wants you to honor Him by telling Him the truth. This isn't because He doesn't know the truth. He does. It's more important to God that you get it. He wants you to understand why you did it, why it's wrong, and why you should not do it again.

All of this and also reassuring you that your sins are forgiven — builds your character and is a critical focus of God's refining work in us.

God uses every aspect of your life, including joy, pain, trouble, illness, achievement, failure, and every other human experience. But in this context, He also uses your sins to hone you, smooth out your rough spots, remove impurities, and gradually make you more like Jesus.

He also wants you to own your sins and mistakes. If you hurt someone, intentionally or not, you owe them an apology. It is also a display of character that God blesses. It is part of loving one another.

Your apology may not be accepted by the person you sinned against. The severity of the wrong and the timing of the apology may prevent that, at least initially. But making a sincere effort is a worthwhile thing to do, whether it is received well or not. God blesses the contrite heart that leads to a pure act of apology.

Contrition

Contrition, which is sometimes equated with a more legal term, remorse, is feeling bad for a mistake or intentional wrong thing you did. You don't just *feel* guilty. You *are* guilty.

This doesn't just apply to solo acts. Sometimes you're in a group that does something wrong. Then there is the extra dimension of peer pressure, which can complicate your efforts to make amends. But your sin and its confession are still between you and God. He knows your role in the sin. He knows if you were a (relatively) innocent bystander. There is no sense in telling God, "It's not my fault." He already knows, either way.

Again, God wants you to "get it." Even if you were innocent, you can still be contrite, and you can feel guilty for not doing something about it before, during, or after the fact. This is when the group aspect of making amends gets difficult, especially for younger people.

Maybe you're with a group, and somebody decides to do something wrong. They want to steal something, break or damage something, or hurt someone. Whatever it is, the idea is raised, there is a quick agreement, and the next thing you know, you're caught up in an incident that moves very fast from the first inkling to it being over and done in a matter of moments.

You can no longer stop it. What's done is done. Your friends may panic and begin planning to cover up what everyone did. They may swear you to secrecy. They may try to pin all the blame on you or someone else.

Depending on the actual deed, law enforcement may get involved. Maybe there are suspensions from school, or expulsions from a team, the loss of a job, a lawsuit, criminal fines, and even jail time. There is a wide range of earthly consequences for our actions and many ways we can be made to answer for our mistakes.

From heaven's perspective, the matter is still between you and God. He is teaching you right from wrong, what character does under stress, owning your mistakes, and telling the truth. Whatever it is, that is why the situation happened. He will use the bad to make for the good of those who love Him.

See **Appendix 6** for prayers asking God for His forgiveness and mercy.

Praying for Wisdom

What Is Wisdom?

Wisdom is spoken about in great breadth and detail in the Bible. King Solomon, the son of King David, was known as the wisest man of his time.

The reason he was so wise was that he had the wherewithal to ask God for wisdom. In fact, when he assumed the throne, God told him he could have anything he asked for. Instead of asking for power or wealth or prestige or fame, Solomon asked for wisdom.

God delivered, as He normally does when a prayer is raised for the right thing and the right reason: lavishly. In his lifetime, Solomon accrued incredible wealth, fame, and prestige. He also wrote the book of Proverbs, part of the Old Testament, and most, if not all, of Ecclesiastes. He also wrote some songs in Songs of Solomon, and he may have written some of Psalms, but the bulk of them were written by his father, David.

Wisdom is the knowledge and understanding of many things, tangible and intangible. It encompasses an understanding of people, of one's strengths and limitations, confidence, humility, prudence, charity, discipline, kindness, and more. It enables one to be a good learner because they know what they need to learn, and they have the discipline to absorb it.

The trait of wisdom and its components reduce the risk of all sorts of disasters in one's life. Being able to understand, plan for, and whenever possible, avoid risks and makes the path straighter and smoother.

Is Wisdom Really So Valuable?

Solomon knew the value of wisdom, both for his own good and for God's glory. Solomon wrote these verses, specifically answering this question:

> *She is more precious than rubies; nothing you desire can compare with her.*
> *Proverbs 3:15 NIV*

> *Do not forsake wisdom, and she will protect you; love her, and she will watch over you.*
> *Proverbs 4:6 NIV*

> *Cherish her, and she will exalt you; embrace her, and she will honor you.*
> *Proverbs 4:8 NIV*

> *For through wisdom your days will be many, and years will be added to your life. If you are wise, your wisdom will reward you; if you are a mocker, you alone will suffer.*
> *Proverbs 9:11–12 NIV*

What Makes Us Think We Will Get Wisdom Just Because We Pray for It?

While Solomon doesn't specify this aspect, James, the apostle, shared this insight that enables us in our search for wisdom:

> *If any of you lacks wisdom, you should ask God, who gives generously to all without finding fault, and it will be given to you. But when you ask, you must believe and not doubt, because the one who doubts is like a*

wave of the sea, blown and tossed by the
wind.
James 1:5–6 NIV

Aside from God Giving His Wisdom Freely, Why Else Would We Want It?

As a practical matter, the possessor of wisdom has a highly leverageable tool. Wisdom enables someone to have the ability to accomplish more important things. In fact, wisdom enables one to accomplish whatever one sets their mind to. This happened to Solomon, and it can happen to those who seek the Lord and His salvation. Along with that comes wisdom.

You can use wisdom in every endeavor you decide to pursue. It's valuable to have in industry, academia, the military, in non-profit work, in personal relationships, and in decision-making of all scopes and environments.

Knowing facts makes you smart, but understanding how facts interrelate and affect conditions and people and the ability to make decisions with that collective knowledge makes you wise.

What Are Some Good Words to Use When Praying for Wisdom?

- Thanks

- Praise

- Clarity

Some Specific Intentions for Things and Words to Pray Them

- Obvious needs vs. Obvious wants

- Physical and Mental Relief

- Renounce sin

- Career or other occupational situation

- Luxury

- Find love

See **Appendix 7** for prayer ideas when praying for Wisdom

Praying for Spiritual Growth

What do you mean by "spiritual growth"?

Spiritual growth refers to the deepening and broadening of one's faith and understanding of the Lord and what He is doing in the world and with us individually. It is the increasing awareness of God's presence in everything you do and everywhere you go.

Once you have decided to become a Christian, that is, to accept the Lord into your life and worship Him, that is the beginning of the journey, not the end. The Holy Spirit, the third person in the trinity that is God, dwells in you when you accept the gifts of the Lord. The Holy Spirit, and His presence, is one of the most important of these gifts.

God will be working on you, helping develop your character, refining your faith, testing you periodically with various challenges, and helping you pass every test you encounter.

He has a plan for your life, and his concept of your life is eternal. You anticipate living for seventy-five to one hundred years on earth. That's a long time, but in the context of eternity, it's a nanosecond. God sees far beyond that barrier and is shaping you not only for this world but for the next. His plan for you is not confined to your life on earth, which may be a reason we find ourselves wondering what on earth 'that' was about. The answer is nothing, on earth anyway.

First things first

Do you accept the gift of eternal life as offered through Jesus Christ? That is a critical question. All other questions are on hold, awaiting your decision.

Hopefully, you say yes to these gifts. They are free, unearned, and far more valuable than anything you have ever given or received.

After I say "yes," and "I'm in," what do I do after that?

Having been saved by the grace of God, you are now one of His people. Nothing you can do for the rest of your life can change that. You have made sure that when the time comes, you will have a home in heaven, where you will be welcomed with open arms.

But does that mean you can relax and slack off, knowing you are saved? Not at all. This, after all, is the start of your journey—the origin, not the destination. It is great you have opened your heart to Jesus. But you owe it to yourself to experience the joy and peace of being with Jesus, and to do that, you must act.

Much of this growth will come naturally, a combination of your growing awareness of God's work in your life and His master plan, which will be 100 percent effective in helping you grow.

But the action you must take is to lean into your spiritual growth. How? By praying for it.

Process for Spiritual Growth

When God is working on you, and you are working on you, your growth and development are assured. But it's always good to pray to the Lord to help you grow and to thank Him for that help. It will help you feel closer to him.

In praying for spiritual growth, you want to ask for the things that expand your growth and move you along more quickly. Be eager for this growth, knowing that every bit of it brings you closer to Jesus.

So pray to the Spirit for the wisdom to understand, the stamina to persevere in trials, the faith to know God is with you, and the confidence to know God will not fail, so you will not fail.

Ask for the strength to obey, even when the test is daunting. Ask for the awareness to recognize His work and His direction. Ask for His clarity, so you are sure you aren't missing anything. Ask for discernment, so you can avoid Satan's lies and schemes that may lead you astray.

The Lord will give you everything you ask for in these prayers since His plan is to give them to you anyway. God is always pleased with our active involvement in the growth of our spirit and faith.

A Caveat

Although the growth of your faith is part of God's plan for your life, it does not mean the process will be easy.

Like most of your education, there will be some things that come more easily to you than others. You may be very compassionate and empathetic but struggle with the nuts and bolts of serving others. You may be very generous and charitable, but you may judge others harshly in some circumstances.

The Lord knows all your strengths and weaknesses, and He knows how He made you to be. Having done that, He knows what your capacity is. So while you may feel comfortable that you are compassionate enough, God may know you still have a long way to go in that area. Likewise, He may not have shaped you for direct service to others, as a nurse, a chef, a customer service rep, or a pastor might be. You might be at your capacity for that sort of service already. He may then look to continue to build on a strength, knowing a weakness is going to stay a weakness for your particular mission.

On the one hand, you could look at this as getting to stay in your comfort zone working on something you're already good at. But realize growth is just that — it's not staying still with what you are right now. Through experiences and opportunities and problems, the Lord will stretch your muscles in the area in which you had thought you were strong enough.

Just as it could be that He could see you as maxed-out on compassion, He may see your capacity for serving others has a lot of room before it fills up. So you may find yourself out of your comfort zone much of the time.

Regardless, whether you are learning something new or building up a particular group of talents, it is work. It can be frustrating, and you may struggle at times. Whether you are struggling or sailing along easily, the Lord is with you, charting your progress, and cheering you on.

Whether the experience is easy and fun or hard and frustrating, He is with you. He is helping you. He wants you to excel as much as you do. And you will. Just follow His lead.

See **Appendix 8** for ideas for praying for Spiritual Growth

15. Praying for the Special Things: Do My Prayers Matter?

Yes

As we alluded to, God will supply all the salvation, forgiveness, wisdom, and spiritual growth we can sincerely ask for, and even if we don't ask for it, He provides it anyway.

These things are special, along with traits like kindness, meekness, and compassion, which are some things that make us more like Jesus. This perfection is the long-term refinement goal for God with every one of His people.

Because these special gifts are in unlimited supply and are, by definition, unable to be used for any intention other than a positive one, they are set apart from other things. Even good things can be overdone, leading to sin, but these cannot.

For those reasons, unlike our other "Do My Prayers Matter?" essays, the only answer to this question regarding special things is an emphatic 'Yes.'

For more on praying for **Salvation**, **Forgiveness**, **Wisdom**, and **Spiritual Growth**, see Appendices 5-8

16. Less Personal Prayers

How Can Prayer be Impersonal?

Very often, we have intentions to pray for people we don't know, sometimes in large groups.

We may pray for the poor, the oppressed, the sick, the government leaders, the police, the first responders, the victims of a hurricane, or war, or some other disaster.

You're not praying for a single person, but a whole group of single persons. Maybe a whole profession, or geographic area, or nation, or the whole world.

Because even though you don't know the people for whom you are praying, you know what their needs are, at least generally. At a minimum, you know they need prayers, and that is enough. And you ask God to help them.

God knows who all the individuals are—even though you don't—and is caring for their needs already.

Ultimately, praying for one little boy who breaks his arm playing tee-ball or the entire human race dealing with an incurable virus pandemic that spreads when people live their normal lives, you are still asking God for help for someone (or many someones) other than yourself.

There Are so Many Problems in the World

It's no secret, we live in a world with many problems. We live in a world that is broken by sin. Evil is loose, and Satan is doing his best to literally wreak havoc. As you can tell by the daily news, he's rather good at it. (That is the only time we will refer to "good" and "Satan" in the same sentence).

Some problems seem like they "just happen." But a closer look at problems like poverty, starvation, war, disease, or injustice will reveal a fundamental component in all of them: Sin.

The sins differ, whether it's greed, envy, prejudice, stubbornness, conceit, hatred, fear, pride, or hundreds of other negative intentions that flow through the hearts of people. Or even of just one person.

When evil is let loose in society, and it isn't immediately corralled and stopped, it's because someone powerful—individuals, small groups, or entire nations—benefits. The status quo is not a problem for them, but it is a problem for someone and possibly everyone else.

People of Good Will Want to Help

Human beings are empathetic. They hear about people in trouble, and to one degree or another, they relate what they hear or see to themselves.

> *"I would be so afraid if wildfires were approaching my home! Thank God, they're not!"*

"Imagine those poor people with COVID-19 unable to have their family visit them when they are so sick!"

"I wish there were something we could do for that family who lost their home and belongings in a fire."

Frequently, this is as far as the empathy gets because unless it's your job to go and help, or if you're right there, there doesn't seem to be much you can do.

Human beings are geographically disbursed, but bad news travels fast. Whenever there is a hurricane, tornado, mass shooting, or the death of a beloved celebrity, millions know it within a few minutes, and most people within a few hours.

The media have become so efficient at delivering a constant stream of news that the average person can't keep up with it.

The overloaded, overwhelmed mind stops reacting when there is too much to react to. We become numb to the suffering because there is so much of it.

Still, people of goodwill want to do "something." Whether they donate money to the Red Cross disaster relief, or something similar, it's easier than ever to do that with smartphones and internet access everywhere.

But the people who have a fleeting thought about helping, because of empathy, shrug it off because "there's nothing I can do about it."

But prayer is something you can *always* do.

Something helpful. Something honest and true and always good. Prayer is a tangible and highly productive assist to those struggling with the problems of the world, whatever the problem, wherever it exists, and whomever it affects.

You don't need special skills, a plane ticket, medical training, or firefighting certification. You don't need money or a credit card. All you need is empathy, the will to help somehow, and an unwillingness to let it go at "there's nothing I can do." Add to that the habit of saying a prayer when you hear about these things, and you can almost consider yourself a first responder.

Ask God to help. Give the best description you have — "God, help the victims of the volcano eruption that destroyed that town." God knows exactly what and where you mean. You need not have longitudes and latitudes to guide Him. You don't have to know how to pronounce the name of the place.

You can even say, "God, help the victims of that disaster I saw a little about on the news. I didn't hear the details, but it seemed a lot of people were suffering. I ask You to help them, in Jesus' name, amen."

God will never be surprised. He will never say, "Hmm, nope, doesn't ring a bell," or "Can you tell me more about it? I can't tell what you're talking about."

You cannot "scoop" the Creator of the Universe. He knows.

He knows your mind and heart, too, as well as everything you have ever seen and heard and read whether you remember or not. He knows what is driving your mind and heart better than you do.

Cynics and Naysayers

There will be cynics in the world who dispute the value or use of prayer. They don't believe because they cannot see. To them, good outcomes come from luck or chance, and bad outcomes are just confirmation that there is no God who cares or loves us.

The important thing is you believe in the power of prayer, and there is a living God who loves us, hears our prayers, and cares for our needs.

Whose needs? Everyone's needs. Even the cynics.

Prayer doesn't take the place of feasible action, but it is a perfect complement to it. If you are on the site of a disaster or otherwise available to help the victims, say a quick prayer that says, "Lord, I'm here for a reason, and I know You want me to help. Show me what to do and how to help and bless my efforts to help these people. In Your name, AMEN." If this seems too long, there is the ever-popular "God, help me!" He will.

Depending on the cynic, you may or may not want to explain your faith. But if possible, the Lord wants you to do it. You may face anger, mockery, or condescension. Don't feel defensive. You have your faith, and they don't have to believe as you do.

But if you can explain how your faith in Jesus has given you peace, comfort, confidence, hope, motivation, or any other positive push, make sure you share that.

Realize a person's faith or lack of it is an accumulation of things. A nonbeliever may not come to Jesus based on one conversation or incident. The depth of their unbelief, pride, or supposed knowledge and education may hold them back. Those factors are from Satan, and they intensify in the face of a call to faith in God.

Be content to be one snowflake on what could become a blizzard. As their life changes, the flakes may fall fast and heavy, and before you know it, you meet them in church on Sunday. They may even acknowledge yours was the first snowflake of their faith storm they saw.

His Will Be Done

Believers know "His will be done," and that includes any outcome whatsoever. God will have His way.

God is not limited to the human definition of *possible*.

We learn the limits of ourselves and those around us at an early age. The word "impossible" is well-known to any kid who is told there is no Santa Claus on the elementary school playground. Our world of limitless possibilities begins to shrink early in life.

God has no limits. He controls everything, including time and space and every single person He ever created. Each one of us is a miracle, though we don't think of ourselves that way. We focus on our flaws, weaknesses, or limitations.

It is that focus that keeps us from doing more. One of our weaknesses may be around faith and trust in God.

"Sure, God can do anything, but He won't do this..."

How do you know?

You don't know. It may not be His will, and so He will not do a particular thing.

His plan is different. And perfect, by the way.

Other times, He will flex His power and deliver something special. Something miraculous. Something that may start a blizzard in that unbeliever's mind. Something that reminds you of who He is. And why you believe Him.

We may never fully (or even partially) understand why the Lord does or does not do something. Likely, we won't.

Remember, He reminded us:

> *"For my thoughts are not your thoughts,*
> *neither are your ways my ways,"*
> *declares the LORD.*
> *Isaiah 55:8 NIV*

17. Less Personalized Prayers – Is God Interested?

Yes

As I write this in September of 2020, the world is battling a pandemic, the likes of which we have never seen.

The COVID-19 pandemic has impacted most countries around the world. Globally, travel has been greatly reduced. Millions of jobs, trillions of dollars, and hundreds of thousands of lives have been lost across the world.

Governments have been all over the map in terms of response. Some have done reasonably well under very ambiguous circumstances. Others have done very poorly.

During this time, many people in many places feel helpless, lost, and indecisive as to what they can or cannot do to keep themselves and their loved ones safe.

Depending on your situation, you will look at this crisis differently. If you own a restaurant or hotel or work for an airline, your livelihood has taken a huge hit. If you are a farmer in western Nebraska, you may be completely unaffected in terms of health, but selling your crops has become impossible.

If you are an intensive care nurse at a big metropolitan hospital, you are on the front lines of the biggest public health crisis in generations. All around you is sickness and death, and a fear of infection that is greater than any the health care system has ever dealt with.

Along with the hard work of a nurse, you are dealing with extra safety protocols, wearing extra protective gear, assuming your hospital has enough for you, and rules that limit patient visitors to reduce the spread. You may have had to postpone vacations or other normal life things to bridge the staffing gap that happens when hospitals are full of dangerously sick people.

And you are the last person someone dying will see since family and friends cannot visit. You may witness, repeatedly, the heartbreak of people dying alone or with a well-meaning stranger holding their hand.

Although I have no data, there is no doubt in my mind that prayer activity has increased during this time. We are dealing with a problem that is global, invisible, and defies understanding. Into this ambiguous, chaotic situation, those same well-meaning, empathetic humans who want to do something are joined by many others, whose needs may be similar, or they may be very different.

The seriously ill patient in the hospital may be praying for healing, or they may be praying for their families if they suspect they're going to die. So many things must run through the mind of a dying person. Hopefully, they pray to the Lord, whom they may soon meet face-to-face. Hopefully, that brings peace and comfort.

The ICU nurse may pray for her dying patient as she holds his hand during his last minutes. How about her safety? How sure is she that she isn't bringing the virus home to her loved ones? What about a colleague who is now a patient struggling with the virus. When did she have lunch with him?

Many things to pray about.

The restaurant owner who invested all her money to start her place is now in the excruciating position of trying to keep it alive when the government has reduced capacity, insisted on outside seating, required strict compliance with protocols, and now winter approaches and outdoor seating will no longer be feasible.

She has a lot of things to pray about.

The school teacher who is required to return to work full-time, in-person, as though the world is normal when it isn't. Do you put yourself at risk? And your family too? What about your colleagues, and what about the students? How do you work? Or do you work? Is this a sign you should find another profession?

He has a lot of prayers to pray, too.

The Nebraska farmer about to lose his family farm after six generations because his yearly crop will waste in silos without a market to buy them. His desperation, misery, and anger are all there, and hopefully, he is speaking to the Lord about the situation.

He, too has a full list to share with the Lord.

Hopefully, they are all comforted by the Lord's direction that:

> *Do not be anxious about anything, but in every situation, by prayer and petition, with thanksgiving, present your requests to God. And the peace of God, which transcends all*

understanding, will guard your hearts and your minds in Christ Jesus.
Philippians 4:6–7 NIV

And:

...I have learned the secret of being content in any and every situation, whether well fed or hungry, whether living in plenty or in want. I can do all this through him who gives me strength.
Philippians 4:12–13 NIV

Part 5
Assembling the Pieces –
Your Action Plan

18. Reading God's Word

Starting a Habit of Reading the Bible

Anyone who has tried to pick up the Bible and read it as one might do with a novel or a newspaper is quickly discouraged.

First, it's not a book. It's a book of books — sixty-six of them. They were written by forty different authors over a span of fifteen hundred or so years. As a result, the books can differ in writing style and terminology. There are several major and many less prevalent translations.

Different books have different purposes:

- Genesis starts off by explaining the origins of the world and of humanity and other facets of God's creation.

- Several more describe the history of the world, of the Israelite people, Israel's kings, her conquerors, her struggles, and her redemptions.

- Others were books of prophets of God.

- The New Testament begins with the birth of Jesus and the four Gospels of Matthew, Mark, Luke, and John, which chronicle Jesus' life, ministry, and teachings.

- After those, the books and letters of the apostles and their work in spreading the gospel to both Jews and Gentiles across the world.

- The last book of the Bible provides a prophecy of the end of this world and the beginning of a new world, entirely ruled by Jesus Christ, from which evil has been banished.

With that many different purposes, topics, and translations, the average person cannot just pick it up and start reading it and feel confident they get it. Some scholars spend their careers trying to "get it" and to help others find their way.

Despite its pure density, the Bible is readable and understandable in many places without further magnification. In addition, more recent translations have sought to provide plain English text, making it a little less daunting to get through. The Message translation is the most prominent of these.

There are many miraculous things about the Bible the casual observer might miss. For one thing, despite the many authors, years, and translations, the Bible never contradicts itself. The consistent line extends from Genesis 1 (or even before) and ends at Revelations 22:21. That common line is Jesus.

Even with regular reading, some miracles of the Bible are well-hidden. The best way to deepen your understanding of God's Word is to follow along with a study Bible, which will provide you insight into historical and cultural contexts, laws and regulations, political climate, wars, dominant nations, prominent leaders, and many other things.

A very small example: the Bible uses the word "yolk" to describe a burden one must carry. There are instances where this is very literal, and others where it is a metaphor.

Regardless, if you're like me, your experience with yolks limited to the yellow part of a chicken egg. So reading about yolks as they were on people, being carried and that sometimes the yolk was heavy was confusing. And it sounded yucky.

At that stage, I didn't know about study Bibles and wasn't rigorous enough to investigate a definition, so I ran along ignorantly until I heard Rick Warren talk about it on his podcast. Very much in passing, so as not to belabor the point, Rick explained a yolk was a device used to keep oxen and other work animals together so

they could pull whatever they were pulling, such as a plow or wagon, as quickly and efficiently as possible.

The yolk fits around the two animals' necks and attaches to whatever they are pulling so they don't run off or cause other delays or damage. [ii]

They look uncomfortable and heavy so but Jesus says:

"Come to me, all you who are weary and burdened, and I will give you rest. Take my yoke upon you and learn from me, for I am gentle and humble in heart, and you will find rest for your souls. For my yoke is easy and my burden is light."
Matthew 11:28–30 NIV

Be Realistic as to How Much You Will Read

To carry the metaphor one last step, keep your yolk is easy and your burden is light as you start reading God's Word.

Realize you are doing something God wants us to do, and that is to learn more about Him through His Word. As we said, He is never in a hurry, so He is happy to have you reading and learning at a pace that makes sense for you and fosters your spiritual growth.

There is no test at the end of the term. Not on the Bible, at least. The Bible provides practical instruction about how God wants us to live our lives. We should worship Him and love one another. There are a lot of variations and subtexts to those two main commands, hence the length and depth of His Word.

In Matthew 6:9–13, Jesus teaches what became known as the Lord's Prayer. It is the first prayer I ever learned as a child. Every night, I recited the memorized lines of this most famous prayer. The meaning of the phrase, "…hallowed be thy name…" was another mystery I never looked at too closely.

These mysteries are part of an important theme when thinking about starting a prayer routine. Going through the motions is a way you can fool yourself into thinking you're growing when you aren't—like the guy who buys nice new running shoes with the idea he would start a running program. But he only wears them to mow the lawn, and he has a ride-on lawnmower. If he thinks he will get in shape by just having the running shoes, he's kidding himself.

Bottom line: it's better to read a couple of verses of God's Word and really think about their meaning than to blast through three pages with no understanding or even questions to ask.

Suggestion: To begin your prayer habit and its Scripture reading component, consider studying Matthew 6:9–13, the Lord's Prayer. Read it a couple of times, then see if you can summarize it in your own words.

It sounds simple, but if you really dig into it, there is a lot of insight in those few words. A sample of that is the first line, "Our Father who is in heaven," Before Jesus, people were terrified of God. They thought Him an angry, vengeful, punitive entity. When Jesus called Him *our Father*, He did a few things:

1. **He shared God with us**. He said OUR Father, not MY Father. We were given fellowship with Jesus and a share of God the Father.

2. When He called God "Father," **He underlined God was not a scary, angry monster to fear and avoid**. Our God is a loving, compassionate, gentle Father who loves all His children. Yes, He is powerful, and we praise Him a couple of lines later when we tell Him His name is hallowed or honored.

3. He disclosed **God is in heaven**, where Jesus came from, and where he would return.

In just six words, Jesus did all that.

And in teaching the prayer to His disciples and by extension to all of us, He gave us direct access to the Father in prayer. People never had that before. This was why the veil tore in the temple when Jesus died. The veil signified the unapproachable nature of God, who couldn't even be approached by priests except in special circumstances. Regular people were kept at a distance.

This is just an example of the endless areas you can drill into in the Bible and find information that is both meaningful to you spiritually and interesting to your mind as well.

Physical or Virtual Bible?

In the old days, Bible readers had to lug around a physical book.

Depending on where and how it was being used, it might have weighed eight to ten pounds.

Paper Bibles had limited space to take notes or add emphasis to passages people wanted to remember.

A lot of Bible readers prefer paper books for their Bible study. If you have a Bible that is special to you or just one you had when you started praying, either way, use what you like and feel comfortable with.

Although the book belongs to you and you can write and mark it up any way you like, if you were ever to pass your Bible along to someone else, they might struggle with your notes, highlights, questions in the margins, and, let's face it, your handwriting. Try to use a notebook to give yourself space to jot down thoughts and insights, questions and confusions, and ideas.

As technology has modernized many other things, so too has it updated and in many ways improved the reading experience with the Bible.

There are websites, smartphone apps, eBooks, workbooks, podcasts, videos of great sermons, and radio broadcasts dedicated not only to the Word of God but also to providing background, scholarly findings, historical and culture context, and interpretation.

For some excellent paper and e-Bibles, as wells as podcasts, videos, and other resources, see **Appendix 1.**

Where to Start?

There are no bad books in the Bible, but some are easier to grasp than others. Just my opinion, but I struggle with numbers, which includes detailed census counts for the various tribes of Israel. Also, everyone is identified by who their father is, as in David, son of Jesse.

- **Gospels** – Matthew, Mark, Luke, and John – These four books encompass Jesus' life, His words, His interactions with others, His example, His miracles, His obedience to His Father, His death, and His resurrection. These are foundational to our faith. All four are wonderful in their own way, but if you want one to start with, **Luke**, to me, is the most detailed.

- When you read these books first, you can see the connection between Jesus' life and various Old Testament texts, where His coming is prophesied numerous times.

- **Acts of the Apostles** – After Jesus ascended to heaven, the eleven disciples (recall that Judas had betrayed Jesus and subsequently committed suicide) were left to figure out what to do next. Jesus sent them to share the gospel with the world, and He gave them His Holy Spirit to stay with them and help them. In addition to all the history, there is suspense, miracles, intrigue, joyful events, and some not so happy events in the building of the early church.

- **Hebrews** – Provides a very condensed summary of most of the Bible. The anonymous writer ties the Old and New Testaments together with Jesus as the common thread.

- **1 and 2 Samuel** – The prophet Samuel was the one through whom God chose David to be King of Israel. His books trace David's story from his anointing by God, to his battle with Goliath, to his time on the run from King Saul, his success in battle, his treachery, and adultery—all woven against the unshakable faith he had and the Lord blessed him for. If David's story were a movie, it would be an epic and a blockbuster if done right.

- **Judges** – for a time, rather than kings, the Israelites were watched over by God-selected men and one woman called judges. These were ordinary people God chose to deliver the Israelites from various dangers. It includes the story of Samson and Delilah, Gideon, and others who transcended their circumstances to deliver the Israelites from death and conquest.

- **Romans** – Especially chapters 7 and 8, which give voice to the human condition (I don't do what I should, but what I shouldn't do? That, I do) and the cure for the human condition, faith in God through Jesus, His Son, who loves us so much we cannot imagine.

- **Psalms** – Psalms looks intimidating with one hundred fifty chapters, but most of these are relatively short poems and songs, mostly written by King David. You will recognize many of them as the words to hymns you've heard before.

- **Proverbs** – King Solomon, son of King David, distinguished himself with his prayer for wisdom, which the Lord gifted to him generously. One of his works is the book of Proverbs that contains a series of short snippets of wisdom about a wide variety of subjects. Altogether, Proverbs is a practical guide to living for the God-believing man or woman.

Other Books for the New Bible Reader

- **Genesis** – "In the beginning God created the heavens and the earth. Now the earth was formless and empty, darkness was over the surface of the deep, and the Spirit of God was hovering over the waters" (Genesis 1:1–2 NIV). These are the famous first words of the Bible. The story of the creation of the world is fascinating and relatively easy to read. Later in Genesis are the stories of Adam and Eve, Noah's Ark, the Tower of Babel, Abram becomes Abraham, and Joseph and the twelve other sons of Isaac.

- **Habakkuk** – A so-called minor prophet, Habakkuk spent almost two-thirds of his three-chapter book laying out his complaints to the Lord. He was unhappy about the injustice and misery being inflicted on the Israelites and the seeming inaction of God. The Lord patiently explains why He is punishing Israel, and He would soon take revenge on the Babylonians, who were battling them at that time. It closes with Habakkuk promising to wait patiently for the "day of calamity to come on the nation invading us."

- **Revelation** – Most people will tell you not to begin any book by reading the end. It spoils it. Not so with the Bible, which concludes with the most terrifyingly awesome story—the end of the world and what comes after. Written by John, the last surviving apostle, it is the vision Jesus gave Him into the end of the earth, the defeat of death and evil, the outcome for believers and nonbelievers, and a glimpse of a new world, ruled by Jesus, free from sin and death. I hope that didn't spoil it for you, but it is a truly incredible crescendo at the end of God's Word.

Wherever you read the Bible, you are reading God's Word, as spoken through His various authors and scribes, prophets, and apostles. Experienced Bible readers report they get new insights every time they reread from various books.

See Appendix 2 for popular verses in scripture, some of which you've heard and some which may be new to you. These may lead you to the chapters and books from which they are taken, another way that your Bible reading habit may be kindled.

19. Five Actions to Build a Happy Prayer Life

Note: There is more to developing a full, well-rounded Christian lifestyle. The focus of this plan is specific to daily prayer and devotional activities. Doing these things alone will transform your life. But there is much more you can do.

1. Invest in a Good Study Bible – Either a Book or an App

A study Bible differs from a regular Bible in that it has notes and insights about the Scriptures to enable the reader to better understand. This helps because the Bible can be tough to read in places, so some guidance from biblical scholars can add a lot to your experience (and lower your frustration).

- Understand the Faith Study Bible – Zondervan

- NLT Christian Basics Bible – Tyndale

- CSB Apologetics Study Bible – B&H

- NIV Cultural Backgrounds Study Bible – Zondervan

- ESV Systematic Theology Study Bible – Crossway

- NKJV Apply the Word Study Bible – Thomas Nelson

- NIV Faith and Work Bible – Zondervan

If you prefer to use an iOS or Android application, here are the two best in my opinion (see details in Appendix B):

- Olive Tree

- Glo Bible

2. If You Commute, Download a Podcast or Two

Podcasts are a great way to use your commute time to get good Bible teaching.

The focus needs to be on what is in the Bible and insights surrounding that, including historical context and what was meant by certain words—not in great detail, but so that you can understand the context the Scripture writer was working in.

For example, when Paul wrote his second letter to Timothy, he was in a Roman prison chained twenty-four hours a day to a Roman centurion (soldier) so that he would not escape. He may have had Luke with him to transcribe his dictation. He wrote the letter knowing his work was completed and his death was near.

That kind of detail, which isn't explicitly included in the text, makes the story come alive and lets you know how hard the apostle worked to ensure the continuity of the faith and capture the wisdom that makes up most of the New Testament.

My two favorite podcasts are:

- *Daily Hope with Rick Warren*, which features a twenty-five-minute sermonette reviewing some aspect of Scripture and its application to our lives.

- *Drivetime Devotions with Tom Holliday*, which is a ten to fifteen-minute daily Bible study, providing insight and encouragement in the reading of God's word.

3. Start a Prayer Journal

My prayer journal IS my prayer life. I have trouble praying to myself, and I am not as comfortable as I would like to be praying out loud. I am also a writer, so typing prayers is right in my comfort zone.

The prayer journal entries are formatted as a letter to God. I date them, so I can look back, and it is a letter where I fill God in on whatever I'm thinking about. It keeps me focused on what I will write about, so I remember to thank and praise God, and I make sure to pray for people who need it. Everybody needs prayer, but some more urgently than others.

Mine is a Microsoft Word document, but you can use other applications or an actual journal book, or just a spiral notebook if you like to write on paper. You could do an audio or video prayer journal, which could develop into a podcast, especially if you included a friend or two.

4. Set a Time

For it to be a routine, you must schedule it. Mine has adjusted due to changes that happen from time to time. I currently get up at six in the morning, get coffee and a bagel, go into my office (at home), and read from the Bible (I use a website) for twenty to thirty minutes. Then I type my letter to God in my journal, which is usually seven hundred fifty to one thousand words or up to two pages.

The beauty of this routine is that it's flexible. If I wake up late or must be somewhere early, I can shorten it, and when I have nothing pressing, I can go longer. The other beauty is time with the Lord, which as you get to doing it consistently, starts to be a need, and you make sure you do it because you enjoy it.

5. Pray any Time

As we have said, you can pray to the Lord any time you want about anything you want, and in any communication mode you like.

If you are going into a difficult meeting at work, say a quick prayer,

> "Lord, thank You for being with me. Help me work well with these people, despite issues in the past, Help me do my part to improve things, In Jesus name, AMEN!"

If you are going home at the end of the day, having started the day with an argument at home, you may not be relishing your return home. Say this:

"God, help me restore peace in my home when I get there. I am sorry I couldn't prioritize love over being right all the time. Help (my spouse) realize (their) part in this, so we might come to a better discussion now that we're calm. Thank You for helping me with this. In Jesus' name, AMEN!"

Incorporating any or all these actions will bolster your prayer life and increase your faith and awareness of God's work in the world. The Lord hears your prayers and answers every one.

Final Thoughts

This book encompasses what I know about prayer and how I have been able to incorporate it in a way that has transformed my life, faith, and hope for the present and for eternity.

I am grateful for your reading it, and I would love to hear feedback and ideas it provoked when you read it. My email address is below.

If I may share just one more thing: as this is a lot of information, it's possible you may sense that prayer really is complicated. After all, why would it take a couple of hundred pages to explain something that's supposed to be simple?

If you feel that way, put the book down and don't pick it up again. Use it for a doorstop or to stop a chair from wobbling.

At the end of all this, there are only two things involved in prayer that really matter:

One is the Creator of the universe, the omnipotent ruler of all there is, anywhere, anytime. The Father, the Son, and the Holy Spirit, the Holy Trinity. God.

The other is you. When you pray, it is only you and God. Remember, He loves you with love so strong you cannot imagine it. The greatest power in all creation is thrilled to be hearing from you. He has time. He has no waiting room or schedule. His attention is on you. His delight is on you. His priority is you. There is nothing He would rather be doing.

So why not start now? Call Him, He's home.

Jim Donaher

Jim@JimDonaher.com

Appendices

Appendix 1 – Great Resources

Books

- Rick Warren, The Purpose Driven Life: What on Earth Am I Here For? (Grand Rapids, MI: Zondervan), 2002.

- KC Hairston, *The Forgotten Rules of Prayer.* (Downers Grove, IL: IVP Books), 2004.

- Sarah Young, Jesus Calling: Enjoying Peace in His Presence. (Thomas Nelson), 2014.

Websites and Articles

Rick Warren, "Home." Pastor Rick's Daily Hope, 2019, pastorrick.com/.

Adriel Sanchez, et al. "True vs. False Repentance: What's the Difference?" Core Christianity, Core Christianity, 25 Sept. 2018, **corechristianity.com/resource-library/articles/true-vs-false-repentance-whats-the-difference**.

"Read and Study the Bible - Daily Verse, Scripture by Topic, Stories." Bible Study Tools, Bible Study Tools, 2019, www.biblestudytools.com/.

Emily Lund, et al. "Top 7 Study Bibles." ChristianBibleStudies.com | Transformed by the Truth, 2017, **www.christianitytoday.com/biblestudies/articles/bibleinsights/top-7-study-bibles.html**.

Podcasts

T. Holliday, (Host) (2019, July 30) "Luke and Acts Week 4, Day 2" [Audio Podcast] Retrieved from http://drivetimedevotions.com/devotions/latest

R. Warren, (Host) (2019, July 30) "How to Rejoice in God's Goodness to Others." [Audio Podcast and Newsletter] Retrieved from **https://pastorrick.com/how-to-rejoice-in-gods-goodness-to-othe**rs-2/

Pope Francis, Holy Father, Pope, Roman Catholic Church, Various topics and dates **https://www.vaticannews.va/en/podcast/the-voice-of-the-pope.html**

C. Groeshel, LifeChurch, Edmond, Oklahoma, (Host) "Leadership Podcast" various dates and topics, https://www.life.church/leadershippodcast/

Great Pastors and Past Messages

P. Atwater, North River Community Church, Pembroke, Massachusetts, various topics and dates, **http://northriverchurch.org/messages/**

T. Dagley, Community Baptist Church, Weymouth, Massachusetts, various dates and topics, **https://www.youtube.com/channel/UClW3fxHzrbSfRIwnsoMiyjg/videos**

M. Kinds, People's Baptist Church, Boston, Massachusetts, **Guest Appearance,** Unity Vancouver YouTube Channel. Topic: You Are Loved; You Are Enough 10/30/2019

C. Groeshel, LifeChurch, Edmond, Oklahoma, various dates and topics, **https://www.life.church/media/messages/**

Pope Francis, Holy Father, Pope, Roman Catholic Church, various topics and dates https://www.vaticannews.va/en/podcast/the-voice-of-the-pope.html

R. Warren, Saddleback Church, Orange County, California, A Faith That Walks Through the Valley of the Coronavirus

Best Study Bibles

1. *The Lucado Encouraging Word Bible*, New International Version Copyright © 2020 by Thomas Nelson

2. *The Blackaby Study Bible*, Copyright © 2006 by Henry T. Blackaby, G. Richard Blackaby, Thomas W. Blackaby, Melvin D. Blackaby, and Norman C. Blackaby.

3. *Holy Bible, New King James Version*, copyright © 1982 by Thomas Nelson, Inc.

4. Understand the Faith Study Bible – Zondervan

5. NLT Christian Basics Bible – Tyndale

6. CSB Apologetics Study Bible – B&H

7. NIV Cultural Backgrounds Study Bible – Zondervan

8. ESV Systematic Theology Study Bible – Crossway

9. NKJV Apply the Word Study Bible – Thomas Nelson

10. NIV Faith and Work Bible – Zondervan

Bible Applications for Phone or Tablet

Olive Tree Bible Software (Olivetree.com) – Olive Tree offers iOS, Android, and desktop versions, both free and premium

Glo Bible (globible.com) – Glo offers iOS and Android apps, the Basic version is free and particularly good. Premium ($) versions available too

Bible Habit Planning Worksheet

Date: _____

Use this **optional** worksheet to keep track of or plan for regular prayer time. If you walk through these questions, you'll have a good plan that can get you started. Don't be intimidated by all the options. Use as much or as little as you need to plan your prayer time.

When Will You Pray?
- ✓ Daily
- ✓ Weekdays
- ✓ Three Days a Week
- ✓ Once a Week

What Time of Day Will You Pray
- ✓ Early morning
- ✓ During my morning commute
- ✓ Lunch time
- ✓ During my evening commute
- ✓ After dinner
- ✓ Before bed

Physical Surroundings (circle all that apply)
- ✓ Indoors

- ✓ Outdoors

- ✓ Public place

- ✓ Private place (e.g. home)

- ✓ Other_____

Materials, Equipment Needed (circle all that apply)

- ✓ Bible (physical book)

- ✓ Study Bible

- ✓ Highlighters

- ✓ Pens or pencils

- ✓ Notebooks

- ✓ Index cards

- ✓ Laptop

- ✓ Bible App

- ✓ Smartphone

- ✓ Internet connection (Wi-Fi or wired)

- ✓ White noise machine

- ✓ Other materials or equipment

- ✓ Music

- ✓ Tape recorder

Will You Have Other People With You (Besides Jesus)?

- ✓ No, just be me and Jesus

- ✓ Yes, I will have (names) as my prayer buddies

What Is Your Prayer Time Agenda? (circle all that apply)

- ✓ Scripture reading – Old Testament

- ✓ Scripture reading – New Testament

- ✓ Journaling

- ✓ Pray out loud

- ✓ Pray silently

- ✓ Pray in writing (like journaling)

- ✓ Praying some other way
  _____

- ✓ The Lord's Prayer

- ✓ The 23rd Psalm

- ✓ Other Psalms

- ✓ Proverbs

- ✓ Other prayer or Scripture
  _____

- ✓ Use a study Bible

✓ Note-taking (e.g. to keep track of insights you have)

✓ Listen to podcast(s) Which one(s)?

_____

✓ Watch or listen to live or recorded video sermons from great pastors **(see Appendix 1 for several good suggestions)**

Prayer Focus for This Week
✓ What do I want to tell God?

_____

✓ What do I want to ask God?

_____

✓ What problem do I need the most help with this week?

_____

_____

✓ Who needs me to pray for them this week?

_____

_____

Remember
- Humble, yet confident; respectful and polite

- God already knows what a sinner you are (in excruciating detail), and He loves you anyway

- No point in trying to fool God

- Don't blame anyone else

- Seek forgiveness

- Talk normally. Don't act; be yourself

- It's reverence, respecting God for who He is

- Be mentally and spiritually present

- If you find your mind wandering...

- Sometimes, you're tired, worried, or sick, and your focus isn't there.

- God knows before you do.

- You need not belabor the activity just to say you did it.

- God appreciates your effort.

- Quality over Quantity

God would rather have two minutes of true connection with you than sixty minutes, fifty-eight of which are spent staring out the window or reading the news online. Wouldn't you?

Despite your errors, omissions, crimes, failures, mistakes, flaws, indiscretions, lies, cheats, and steals, He loves you more than you could ever, EVER imagine.

Prayer Life SMART Goals Worksheet

Today's Date: _____

- **S-pecific** – You want to develop a prayer habit. What do you mean by that?

- **M-easurable** – You have a goal. How will you know you have achieved it or are making progress?

- **A-ttainable** – Is your goal something you can realistically reach? If not, you're setting yourself up for disappointment

- **R-elevant** – Is this goal aligned with your beliefs and values?

- **T-ime-Based** – Without a time limit, everything (and nothing) is possible.

Specific

What do you want to achieve, exactly? How do you measure that?

_____

_____

_____

What outcome are would you like to see? How do you measure that?

_____

_____
_____
_____

What benefits will YOU receive from the achievement of this goal?

_____
_____
_____

Who else might benefit from your achievement of this goal? How?

_____
_____
_____

Measurable

Do you wish to measure frequency or duration? Use hours, days, weeks, or months?

_____

Do you wish to measure your consistency with a behavior/habit? Use consecutive days, weeks, months, or x out of y days in z month.

_____

Attainable

Remember, God is pleased you are setting out on this project. His timeframe is eternal. He will help you. Just don't psyche yourself out by saying you will read the Bible in a weekend. Even if you do, you won't get much out of it. Take your time.

_____

Are you very enthusiastic about this goal? Good! Just make sure you are realistic about what you can achieve. There is no law that says you can't demolish your goal! Just don't set it so high that you will disappoint yourself when you can't hit it.

Relevant

In what ways will completing this goal bring you closer to the Lord?

_____

_____

_____

Time-Based

By when do you want to complete this goal?

_____

Appendix 2 – Favorite Scripture Readings

Below are some of my favorite Bible verses. Some are iconic and easily recognized; others are hidden gems.

Some of the Most Famous

"For God so loved the world that he gave his one and only Son, that whoever believes in him shall not perish but have eternal life."
John 3:16 NIV

"And we know that in all things God works for the good of those who love him, who have been called according to his purpose."
Romans 8:28 NIV

"In the beginning God created the heavens and the earth."
Genesis 1:1 NIV

"...in all your ways submit to him, and he will make your paths straight."
Proverbs 3:6 NIV

"Do not be anxious about anything, but in every situation, by prayer and petition, with thanksgiving, present your requests to God."
Philippians 4:6 NIV

"For I know the plans I have for you," declares the LORD, "plans to prosper you and not to

harm you, plans to give you hope and a future."
Jeremiah 29:11 NIV

"I can do all this through him who gives me strength."
Philippians 4:13 NIV

"Trust in the LORD with all your heart and lean not on your own understanding..."
Proverbs 3:5 NIV

"Do not conform to the pattern of this world, but be transformed by the renewing of your mind. Then you will be able to test and approve what God's will is—his good, pleasing and perfect will."
Romans 12:2 NIV

My dear children, I write this to you so that you will not sin. But if anybody does sin, we have an advocate with the Father—Jesus Christ, the Righteous One. He is the atoning sacrifice for our sins, and not only for ours but also for the sins of the whole world.
1 John 2:1–2 NIV

Old Testament

"Be strong and courageous. Do not be afraid or terrified because of them, for the LORD your God goes with you; he will never leave you nor forsake you."
Deuteronomy 31:6 NIV

"Saul died because he was unfaithful to the LORD; he did not keep the word of the LORD and even consulted a medium for guidance, and did not inquire of the LORD. So the LORD put him to death and turned the kingdom over to David son of Jesse."
1 Chronicles 10:13–14 NIV

"That day David first appointed Asaph and his associates to give praise to the LORD in this manner: Give praise to the LORD, proclaim his name; make known among the nations what he has done. Sing to him, sing praise to him; tell of all his wonderful acts. Glory in his holy name; let the hearts of those who seek the LORD rejoice. Look to the LORD and his strength; seek his face always. Remember the wonders he has done, his miracles, and the judgments he pronounced, you his servants, the descendants of Israel, his chosen ones, the children of Jacob. He is the LORD our God; his judgments are in all the earth."
1 Chronicles 16:7–14 NIV

"Give thanks to the LORD, for he is good; his love endures forever. Cry out, 'Save us, God our Savior; gather us and deliver us from the nations, that we may give thanks to your holy name, and glory in your praise.'"
1 Chronicles 16:34–35 NIV

"From there Elisha went up to Bethel. As he was walking along the road, some boys came out of the town and jeered at him. "Get out of

here, baldy!" they said. "Get out of here, baldy!" He turned around, looked at them and called down a curse on them in the name of the LORD. Then two bears came out of the woods and mauled forty-two of the boys. And he went on to Mount Carmel and from there returned to Samaria."
2 Kings 2:23–25 NIV

"So do not fear, for I am with you;
do not be dismayed, for I am your God.
I will strengthen you and help you;
I will uphold you with my righteous right hand."
Isaiah 41:10 NIV

"The Lord is my light and my salvation; whom shall I fear? The Lord is the stronghold of my life; of whom shall I be afraid?"
Psalm 27:1 NIV

"There is no peace," says the LORD, "for the wicked."
Isaiah 48:22 NIV

"There is no peace," says my God, "for the wicked." (Yes, he said it in two different places)
Isaiah 57:21 NIV

New Testament – The Gospels

"Therefore go and make disciples of all nations, baptizing them in the name of the Father and of the Son and of the Holy Spirit."

Matthew 28:19 NIV

"Come to me, all you who are weary and burdened, and I will give you rest."
Matthew 11:28 NIV

"Therefore I tell you, do not worry about your life, what you will eat or drink; or about your body, what you will wear. Is not life more than food, and the body more than clothes? Look at the birds of the air; they do not sow or reap or store away in barns, and yet your heavenly Father feeds them. Are you not much more valuable than they? Can any one of you by worrying add a single hour to your life?"
Matthew 6:25–27 NIV

*"Blessed are the poor in spirit,
for theirs is the kingdom of heaven.*

*Blessed are they who mourn,
for they shall be comforted.*

*Blessed are the meek,
for they shall inherit the earth.*

*Blessed are they who hunger and thirst for righteousness,
for they shall be satisfied.*

*Blessed are the merciful,
for they shall obtain mercy.*

*Blessed are the pure of heart,
for they shall see God.*

Blessed are the peacemakers,
for they shall be called children of God.

Blessed are they who are persecuted for the sake of righteousness,
for theirs is the kingdom of heaven."
Matthew 5:3–10 ('The Beatitudes') NIV

The New Testament (Paul's Letters)

"Therefore we do not lose heart. Though outwardly we are wasting away, yet inwardly we are being renewed day by day. For our light and momentary troubles are achieving for us an eternal glory that far outweighs them all. So we fix our eyes not on what is seen, but on what is unseen, since what is seen is temporary, but what is unseen is eternal."
2 Corinthians 4:16–18 NIV

"…Therefore, in order to keep me from becoming conceited, I was given a thorn in my flesh, a messenger of Satan, to torment me. Three times I pleaded with the Lord to take it away from me. But he said to me, "My grace is sufficient for you, for my power is made perfect in weakness." Therefore I will boast all the more gladly about my weaknesses, so that Christ's power may rest on me. That is why, for Christ's sake, I delight in weaknesses, in insults, in hardships, in persecutions, in difficulties. For when I am weak, then I am strong."
2 Corinthians 12:7–10 NIV

"But the fruit of the Spirit is love, joy, peace, forbearance, kindness, goodness, faithfulness, gentleness and self-control. Against such things there is no law. Those who belong to Christ Jesus have crucified the flesh with its passions and desires. Since we live by the Spirit, let us keep in step with the Spirit. Let us not become conceited, provoking, and envying each other."
Galatians 5:22–25 NIV

"Each one should test their own actions. Then they can take pride in themselves alone, without comparing themselves to someone else, 5 for each one should carry their own load. Each one should test their own actions. Then they can take pride in themselves alone, without comparing themselves to someone else, for each one should carry their own load."
Galatians 6:4–5 NIV

"Let us not become weary in doing good, for at the proper time we will reap a harvest if we do not give up. Therefore, as we have opportunity, let us do good to all people, especially to those who belong to the family of believers."
Galatians 6:9–10 NIV

"But because of his great love for us, God, who is rich in mercy, made us alive with Christ even when we were dead in transgressions—it is by grace you have been saved."

Ephesians 2:4–5 NIV

"Get rid of all bitterness, rage and anger, brawling and slander, along with every form of malice. Be kind and compassionate to one another, forgiving each other, just as in Christ God forgave you."
Ephesians 4:31–32 NIV

"Since you died with Christ to the elemental spiritual forces of this world, why, as though you still belonged to the world, do you submit to its rules: "Do not handle! Do not taste! Do not touch!"? These rules, which have to do with things that are all destined to perish with use, are based on merely human commands and teachings. Such regulations indeed have an appearance of wisdom, with their self-imposed worship, their false humility and their harsh treatment of the body, but they lack any value in restraining sensual indulgence."
Colossians 2:20–23 NIV

"You used to walk in these ways, in the life you once lived. But now you must also rid yourselves of all such things as these: anger, rage, malice, slander, and filthy language from your lips. Do not lie to each other, since you have taken off your old self with its practices and have put on the new self, which is being renewed in knowledge in the image of its Creator."
Colossians 3:7–10 NIV

"But mark this: There will be terrible times in the last days. People will be lovers of themselves, lovers of money, boastful, proud, abusive, disobedient to their parents, ungrateful, unholy, without love, unforgiving, slanderous, without self-control, brutal, not lovers of the good, treacherous, rash, conceited, lovers of pleasure rather than lovers of God—having a form of godliness but denying its power. Have nothing to do with such people."
2 Timothy 3:1–5 NIV

"Since an overseer manages God's household, he must be blameless—not overbearing, not quick-tempered, not given to drunkenness, not violent, not pursuing dishonest gain. Rather, he must be hospitable, one who loves what is good, who is self-controlled, upright, holy and disciplined."
Titus 1:7–8 NIV

"Remind the people to be subject to rulers and authorities, to be obedient, to be ready to do whatever is good, to slander no one, to be peaceable and considerate, and always to be gentle toward everyone."
Titus 3:1–2 NIV

New Testament – Apostles and Unknown Authors

"...but because Jesus lives forever, he has a permanent priesthood. Therefore he is able to save completely those who come to God

through him, because he always lives to intercede for them. Such a high priest truly meets our need—one who is holy, blameless, pure, set apart from sinners, exalted above the heavens. Unlike the other high priests, he does not need to offer sacrifices day after day, first for his own sins, and then for the sins of the people. He sacrificed for their sins once for all when he offered himself. For the law appoints as high priests men in all their weakness; but the oath, which came after the law, appointed the Son, who has been made perfect forever."
Hebrews 7:24–28 NIV

"Therefore, since we are receiving a kingdom that cannot be shaken, let us be thankful, and so worship God acceptably with reverence and awe, for our God is a consuming fire."
Hebrews 12:28–29 NIV

"So do not throw away your confidence; it will be richly rewarded. You need to persevere so that when you have done the will of God, you will receive what he has promised. For, "In just a little while, he who is coming will come and will not delay." And, "But my righteous one will live by faith. And I take no pleasure in the one who shrinks back." But we do not belong to those who shrink back and are destroyed, but to those who have faith and are saved."
Hebrews 10:35–39 NIV

"Speak and act as those who are going to be judged by the law that gives freedom, because judgment without mercy will be shown to anyone who has not been merciful. Mercy triumphs over judgment."
James 2:12–13 NIV

"Brothers and sisters, do not slander one another. Anyone who speaks against a brother or sister or judges them speaks against the law and judges it. When you judge the law, you are not keeping it, but sitting in judgment on it. There is only one Lawgiver and Judge, the one who is able to save and destroy. But you—who are you to judge your neighbor?"
James 4:11–12

"Therefore confess your sins to each other and pray for each other so that you may be healed. The prayer of a righteous person is powerful and effective."
James 5:16

If they have escaped the corruption of the world by knowing our Lord and Savior Jesus Christ and are again entangled in it and are overcome, they are worse off at the end than they were at the beginning. It would have been better for them not to have known the way of righteousness, than to have known it and then to turn their backs on the sacred command that was passed on to them. Of them the proverbs are true: "A dog returns to

its vomit," and, 'A sow that is washed returns to her wallowing in the mud.'"
2 Peter 2:20–22

"But do not forget this one thing, dear friends: With the Lord a day is like a thousand years, and a thousand years are like a day. The Lord is not slow in keeping his promise, as some understand slowness. Instead he is patient with you, not wanting anyone to perish, but everyone to come to repentance."
2 Peter 3:8–9

"Everyone who sins breaks the law; in fact, sin is lawlessness. But you know that he appeared so that he might take away our sins. And in him is no sin. No one who lives in him keeps on sinning. No one who continues to sin has either seen him or known him."
1 John 3:4–5

"This is how we know who the children of God are and who the children of the devil are: Anyone who does not do what is right is not God's child, nor is anyone who does not love their brother and sister."
1 John 3:10

"Do not be surprised, my brothers and sisters, if the world hates you."
1 John 3:13

"Dear friends, if our hearts do not condemn us, we have confidence before God and receive from him anything we ask, because we keep

his commands and do what pleases him. And this is his command: to believe in the name of his Son, Jesus Christ, and to love one another as he commanded us. The one who keeps God's commands lives in him, and he in them."
1 John 3:21–24

"And now, dear lady, I am not writing you a new command but one we have had from the beginning. I ask that we love one another. And this is love: that we walk in obedience to his commands. As you have heard from the beginning, his command is that you walk in love."
2 John 1:5–6

Appendix 3 –Prayers for People

People are different. While this isn't exactly news, it affects the content of your prayers. Are you praying for someone you love? Are you praying for a single person or a group? Is it someone who hurt you or who you hurt?

These factors make a difference in what you will ask of God. When you pray for someone, you are committing an act of selfless love. In some instances, this will be someone you love in the earthly sense. Your spouse, friends, and family members are people who you love.

In some instances, you will pray for people you do not necessarily know. Praying for the homeless, for people trapped in a war zone, or caught in a terrible storm, or some other environmental catastrophe is also an act of love. You are giving your empathy and making sure they are not alone. This is loving in a heavenly sense.

God also calls on us to pray for and forgive those who hurt us or someone we care about. He also wants us to pray for criminals and other societal outcasts. This may be the hardest kind of prayer, given that you have opinions on the nature of criminals, and you have been personally affected by whoever hurt you.

It isn't the prayer that's the hard part, though. It's the forgiveness and softening of your heart that you need to pray credibly for someone who does harm and who may not even care or acknowledge the victims.

When we go to God in prayer, we can be angry or upset about a situation. God can handle your intensity. Being respectful and reverent doesn't require you to swallow your feelings. God knows how you feel and isn't fazed by anger, frustration, or confusion. Try to take a deep breath and then tell Him what you would like.

For My Spouse

Your spouse is your life partner and your best friend. You know them better than anyone else, and they know you better than anyone else. You know everything about them, including where they struggle, what makes them happy or sad, what they hope and dream of, as well as what, if anything, they fear.

Knowing all this can make praying for your spouse challenging. Remember, prayer is not a "one and done" proposition. You should pray every day. That does not mean you have to pray for every issue facing every person every time you pray. It is too much, and you won't remember it all anyway.

Though many of us want to be the one who "makes it all better" in real life, sometimes, we are limited in what we can do.

The good news on that front is you can pray for them, which we said earlier is one of the strongest acts of love you can do for another person.

God doesn't need you to provide all the details. He already knows and is already working on a solution. If you are to help solve whatever it is, trust God to put you in the right position with whatever you need to do your part.

He likes you to pray, depending on and trusting Him. It is a critical part of your growing relationship with Him.

Below are some ideas about praying for your spouse when they are struggling and discouraged.

Dear God,
Thank You for the chat I just had with (spouse name). (They) are so discouraged, and (they) feel there are no good options.

(They) have trouble getting outside (their) box sometimes and is pushed by the memory of parents or grandparents, who, despite much misery, never complained and never stopped working.

I don't know what to say about that, but I think our life is different, just as theirs were. (Spouse name) has their own path, and they're on it. And You are right there with them. It is not the same as the path of anyone else.

(Spouse name) is in a darker part of the journey now, where (they) can't see the road ahead. It's stressful and requires trust that You are with them, You know what's ahead, and this part of the journey will only last as long as it has to before You get to the next stop.

(They) must trust You to lead them there. That is the test, and it is a tough one. But You want

them to pass, so please, Lord, You can give them the answers. It's still not easy, though.

Bless and keep (Spouse name) calm and focused so that they don't worry or despair. Help them to truly grasp the peace that trust in You brings, knowing that despite our struggles in the here-and-now, You are working all things out for the good of those who love You, and (spouse name) loves You very much.

Thank You for blessing my life with this wonderful partner.

Thank You for bringing us together so many years ago.

Help me to support, love, and care for them every day.

In Jesus' name, I pray, Amen!

For My Friends

One of the greatest blessings in life is to have friends.

Regardless of your age or economic status, and no matter where you are from or where you are going, friends remind you of who you are.

Some childhood friends remember you when you were not as proficient as you are now. They know that regardless of your position on top of the world, they will help keep your ego in check, maintain your humility, and remember that friendship is the glue that keeps life together.

Below are some ideas for praying on behalf of friends. There are a few scenarios, but even if they don't apply, it's good to thank God for your friends.

For Friends Celebrating

Oh, Lord,
Thank You for (friend's name/s) as we celebrate their (graduation, marriage, new baby, victory, success, retirement, etc.).

Thank You for blessing the hard work/diligence/persistence, love, and prayer they put into this effort. I know they are overjoyed, and I am happy that my friend is happy.

Thank You for this wonderful friend and for being able to share in their joyful time.
In the name of Jesus, my best friend, I pray, AMEN!

For Broken-hearted Friends

Dear Lord,
Thank You for my friend (name). You know, they suffered a setback this week, and a lot of their plans fell through because of (some general description of the cause).

Lord, You bless us with friendship out of a desire to see your children work, play, and live together.

One aspect of friendship is empathy born out of history together, shared joys and sorrows, great joy and great disappointment, and the everyday drudgery that is the majority of our days and nights.

Lord, I pray for my friend (name) as they have had this setback, and they are taking it awfully hard. Help those of us who are their friends to come together to support and help them through this sadness.

Lord, bless all our friends.

Thank You for helping us learn empathy, kindness, and friendship in part through this painful incident. This is another example of Your doing a good work out of bad for those who love You.

In Jesus' healing name, I pray, AMEN!

When a Friendship Is Broken

Dear God,
Thank You for the friendship with which You have blessed me with (Name of Friend).

Unfortunately, due to a (disagreement/misunderstanding/mistake), we are not getting along, nor can we address the problem, heal, and move on.

Lord, I value this friendship, and I am sorry this problem occurred. Help me apologize for my part in this and not be prideful. Give me the humility to admit my mistakes and to ask forgiveness from anyone I hurt, especially dear friends like (name of friend).

Let me forgive, whether they choose to apologize or not. Let me be an example of grace and mercy, not holding a grudge, especially with someone like (name of friend) who has been such a good friend.

Lord, I thank You for healing this wound in my friendship with (Name of friend). Thank you for the blessing of a great person who has added richness to my life, and hopefully, I have done the same for them.

In Jesus' name, I pray, AMEN!

For Myself

A lot of us neglect to pray for ourselves. Our needs, fears, and struggles often don't make the cut when it comes to our precious prayer time. You know you have needs and things you want that you cannot get on your own. You know this about other people, too, and you pray for them. Why aren't you praying for yourself?

Maybe you tell yourself you're humble, or you are not worthy. Who gets to speak to the Lord of all things everywhere and talks about their needs? And why does an unworthy person even get in line, except to plead on behalf of others?

(Answer – everyone should.)

It bears repeating that God knows your needs, and He is already working on delivering them, along with at least some of your wants. He loves and cares for you just as much as the people for whom you pray. And He wants you to trust Him to come through for you since He always has and always will.

> *"I have told you these things, so that in me you may have peace. In this world, you will have trouble. But take heart! I have overcome the world."*
> **John 16:33 NIV**

When I Am Overwhelmed

We all have times when life gangs up on us. It usually happens when simultaneous crises demand our attention in several areas of life. You may have a career problem, an elderly parent who needs full-time care, your child being bullied at school, all at the same time when you are two months late on your mortgage and dodging calls from the bank, and the tension between you and your spouse is about to explode. You don't know where to turn.

Turn to God.

> *Dear God,*
> *I am so relieved to be able to talk to You. You always help me settle down and focus on what really matters. I need that every day, but today especially.*
>
> *I am at my wit's end. I cannot seem to get organized to handle everything coming at me.*

My family, my job, my finances, and my marriage all seem to be approaching a crisis at the same time.

You know all the things I am facing (You can list them if you wish). You know how it ends, and who will help me get there (and who will try to stop me).

Lord, I am letting go. I know I can't get this settled down on my own. I will do what I can, but I know this all comes down to You. I know You will deliver me from this when the time is right, so I will be patient and do my best in the meantime.

Jesus, please let me stay close to You; help me make good decisions about how I can spend my time so it can all be taken care of.

When I get like this, I freeze, unable to focus on one task at a time, resulting in slow progress and minimal quality—the exact opposite of what I need to do. My priorities disappear, and I am flailing about, getting nowhere.

Lord, I am so grateful for Your hearing me and Your assurance that You have the situation under control. I trust this as much as I am able, and I know You're teaching me to increase my trust in You. It is more than it was, but it's not as much as it will be someday. I will keep fighting.

I love You,

In Jesus' holy name, I pray, AMEN!

For the Sick or Injured

Very often, we want to pray for someone we know who is either sick or has been injured somehow. There is a very wide range of severity of these things, ranging from a case of the sniffles to a terminal illness or a debilitating accident that changes a life forever.

In this section, we present some scenarios and prayer ideas that may help in that instance. They are purposely vague, so you can apply them to a variety of situations. You can incorporate details as the need fits.

For Multiple People

Sometimes it seems like there are a lot of people who are sick or injured. From a flu epidemic to an accident with multiple people injured to plain dumb luck, you may find you have a list of people to remember in prayer.

> *Dear Lord,*
> *Thank You for being the ultimate healer, providing relief to those of us who get sick or hurt and can't do what we normally do.*
>
> *Thank You for the healing You have brought to my life and those around me. We are incredibly grateful!*
>
> *Lord, I ask Your blessings for these friends, colleagues, and family members who are battling various sicknesses or injuries: (list those for whom you want to pray).*

Bless them with skilled, compassionate care, love, and support from their families and friends, success in their treatments, and relief and healing from pain and suffering.

In Jesus' name, I pray, AMEN!

For a Person with Serious Illness or Injury

Dear Lord,
Thank You for always being with us, giving us guidance, direction, and loving us with Your incomparable, unfailing love.

Thank You for hearing my prayers and for loving us so much.

Lord, I am praying today, especially for (name of the person you're praying for), who is suffering from (specific illness or injury) and is in tough shape.

Bless them with outstanding care, full of compassion, knowledge, and skill. Bless their family and friends, and let them come visit to support, pray, and keep their spirits up.

Soothe their pain, allay their fears, and let them heal and recover so they can go on with their lives. Thank You for hearing me and for Your perfect care for our friend, (name).

In Jesus' healing name, I pray, AMEN!

For A Person with a Terminal Illness or Injuries from Which They Are Unlikely to Recover

Lord,

Your ways are perfect. Your timing is perfect, and Your love for us is beyond our ability to understand. We know this life is not the end, and thus, You take us from this world when the time is right.

It seems time is approaching for our friend (name). They are suffering from (specific illness or injury), and it doesn't look good.

Until the time You choose to bring them home, comfort them with the knowledge You are with them, they are never alone, and they will be coming with You when that time arrives.

Let them have visitors who will pray for them and cheer them up where they can.

Lord, help them realize what is happening and to tell those closest to them that they love and appreciate them, so there are no things left unsaid.

If a miraculous recovery is not Your will, let them pass peacefully, without pain or worry, and with the hopeful expectation of eternal life, which is only available because of Your mercy and Your sacrifice on the cross.

Thank You for hearing my prayers and for caring for (name) as they approach the end of their time here on earth. Thank You for the pleasure of (knowing, working with, being friends with, etc.) our friend (name).

In the mighty name of Jesus, I pray, AMEN!

For A Person Paralysed or Otherwise Seriously Injured in an Accident

Dear Lord,
We don't always understand why things happen. In fact, when they are bad things, especially those that happen to good people, we are especially confused.

"Why them?" we ask when what we mean is, "If it can happen to (them), can it happen to me too?" We feel for the victim and fear that, one day, the victim could be us.

Lord, thank You for saving (name) from the serious injuries (they) suffered in the accident.

Thank You for the first responders who stabilized them and brought them to the hospital.

Thank You for the emergency staff who assessed their condition, made decisions, and took lifesaving action.

Without these wonderful professionals, the accident could easily have been fatal for (name).

Thank You for blessing (name) with survival from such an awful accident. We know that, regardless of our situation, You love us and will always provide for our needs.

We ask Your special care for (name), who will have many struggles adjusting to this new life. Let them surrender their lives to You, as You are the only One who can create good out of a tragedy like this.

We know You will do Your work on them whether they accept in faith the gifts You promise us.

Let those results provide a realization that You are working on their behalf, both directly and through the professionals who care for and rehabilitate them. You will make good out of this bad, in Your perfect timing.

Accepting this in faith and genuinely believing provides us with hope, comfort, and gratitude.

In Jesus' name, AMEN!

For Anyone Struggling

Life involves struggle. No one escapes it.

Your struggles are unique to you, and mine is unique to me. Jesus said in this life, you will have trouble. He didn't say you may, or you could, or you might. He said you will have trouble. (See John 16:33.)

But He also immediately gave us a reason for hope. Because He has overcome the world, those who are in Him and have believed in Him as the Lord of all have overcome it too. It doesn't exempt us from trouble, struggle, problems, or worries. But it does give us a reason to hope. It won't always be this way. In heaven, these things don't exist.

So why do we have to have trouble? The Lord is working on you, refining you, and building your character, integrity, morals, and ethics. Trouble and struggle, unfortunately, are particularly good teachers. Therefore, He allows them.

Below is an idea for praying for individuals, groups, and even the whole world since we all struggle with something.

For more emphasis, use this verse from Paul's letter to the Romans:

> *"And we know that in all things God works for the good of those who love Him, who have been called according to His purpose."*
> **Romans 8:28 NIV**

For Anyone Going Through A Lot
This is someone who is overwhelmed in a way like when you prayed for yourself when you were overwhelmed. They have too many crises, not enough help, and they're left feeling like they're fighting a family of dragons all at once.

Dear God,

Please bless (name of person or group) who has/have been struggling so much of late.

I know they are discouraged and feeling beaten up by circumstances outside their control. When I think about the list of tragedies, setbacks, and disappointments they have suffered, it breaks my heart.

I know You are using these struggles to build them up, and You always make all things work out for the good of those who love you. I hope they know this too, and if they don't, I will have the occasion to share it with them.

I am so grateful for the hope You give us in Your Word. Thank You for encouraging us and letting us know there is a point to all this suffering. You are not punishing us; that is the work of the enemy.

But you allow trouble in the world to refine and improve us as You will through eternity, to be more like Jesus. We learn and grow through these struggles, and that alone is a reason to celebrate.

Thank You, Lord, for hearing my prayer.

In Jesus' name, I pray, AMEN.

For People Grieving

Grief is an emotion unknown to us until we suffer the loss of someone we love. The finality of death is painful and overwhelming, regardless of the circumstances, and we are often at a loss to sort out our feelings, especially if the loss is sudden or unexpected.

In this section are some ideas for praying for those grieving. They are purposely general. Details about a particular situation can be incorporated if desired.

Grieving for a Spouse

Dear Lord,

We are so blessed to have the hope of resurrection and eternal life with You in heaven. This hope provides immense comfort to us, particularly when we lose someone we love.

Sometimes, we have many years of marriage; other times, we may only get a few months. But whatever time we have, we are grateful to You for the gift of our relationship and for the love we share.

Lord, I ask You to bring this comfort and reassurance to (name), whose husband/wife, name) recently left this world to be with You in heaven.

Comfort (name) with sympathetic family, friends, neighbors, and colleagues and for as much or as little company as they can handle at this difficult time.

Most important, comfort (name) with happy memories of good times and excellent experiences. And, grant (name) the comfort and the confidence to know they will see (spouse's name) again when they go to heaven. And what a joyful reunion that will be!

In the loving name of Jesus, I pray, AMEN!

Grieving for a Parent

Dear God,
When we enter this world, You bless us with mothers and fathers.

Sometimes these are our birth parents, other times, we are raised by others, who perform the functions of mothers and fathers: teaching us right from wrong, how to take care of ourselves, how to be a friend, and a million other important things. Thank You for parents who love us and whom we love so much as well.

Lord, bring Your sympathetic shoulder to (name), whose (mother or father) recently left this world to return to heaven to be with You.

Let (name) be comforted by the loving support of family, colleagues, and friends, all of whom provide unique ways of supporting those who grieve.

Let them be further comforted by the confidence that (parent name) has gone home to be with You, that they are safe and out of danger and pain, and are awaiting a joyful reunion with (name) in heaven.

Thank You for this hope, which makes hard times like this a little easier to bear.

In the comforting name of Jesus, I pray, AMEN!

Grieving for a Child

Dear Lord,
When You bless us with children, we consider them ours because we raise them, teach them, protect them, comfort them, discipline them, and prepare them for life. This is understandable, but it ignores the fact that children, like everyone else, belong to You.

You choose us to be the parent of a child, and Your judgment is perfect. Despite how overwhelming the responsibility it is, You guide and help us, and in so doing, You develop three souls at once—the child and their parents.

We assume our children will outlive us, but at times like this, we recognize that any time might be the last time for any of us. We trust in Your judgment and timing, but we are left feeling awful anyway.

Lord bless (name of the parents) who have lost their child (child's name). I ask that You heal *their shattered hearts and comfort them with happy memories and the knowledge that (child's name) is with You—safe and out of pain, anger, and sorrow.*

Thank You, Lord, for surrounding (parent's names) with family and friends, who support and grieve with them, and the kindnesses that will be extended to them as they grieve.

Most importantly, thank You for the reassurance they will see (child's name) again when their time on earth is over.

Bless and keep (parents and siblings' names) renewing their faith and helping them to heal.

In the loving name of Jesus, I pray, AMEN!

Grieving a Miscarriage

Dear Lord,
Watch over and comfort (parent's names) on the miscarriage of their baby.

We know all things happen for a reason, and quite often, we can't see what that reason is. This is such a time. At times like this, some become angry with You, and others withdraw. Let this not happen to (parent's names).

Let them be comforted in that Your timing is always perfect, Your love for them and the baby is unending, and the baby is back at home in heaven—safe, happy, and in no pain.

Lord, heal (mother's name) from the physical and emotional scars of this loss. Bless (father's name) with compassion, love, and care for his wife. Let them help one another to grieve and look to You for hope and consolation.

Help (parent's names) draw close to You and understand Your love and timing—though sometimes hard to see in our grief—are the things that make our lives livable, even at sad times like this.

Let them have or develop trust in You as You always work even bad things out for the good of those who love you. Thank You for Your reassurance and the comfort it brings to us.

In the holy name of Jesus, I pray, Amen.

For Enemies, Rivals, and Criminals

Jesus tells us that we must pray for our enemies. Jesus also spent much of His time with those considered criminals and undesirable by the standards of so-called decent society. Far from shunning these undesirable characters, He regularly ate meals with them! This upset the Pharisees and other respected members of society very much.

Despite that, in our broken world, it sometimes seems almost acceptable to vilify and hate their enemies and to judge and despise criminals of all kinds with special animosity toward the more heinous crimes. This hatred and prejudgment often occur long before any actual trial based on facts occurs.

Below are some ideas for praying to the Lord on behalf of "enemies" as well as for the accused perpetrators of crimes. Praying for our enemies seems antithetical to our view of ourselves as soldiers fighting enemies or as victims of crime against you or someone you love. That is what makes this command from Jesus so challenging. He didn't say it was easy:

> You have heard that it was said, "Love your neighbor and hate your enemy." But I tell you, love your enemies and pray for those who persecute you, that you may be children of your Father in heaven. He causes his sun to rise on the evil and the good, and sends rain on the righteous and the unrighteous. If you love those who love you, what reward will you get? Are not even the tax collectors doing that? And if you greet only your own people, what are you doing more than others? Do not even pagans do that? Be perfect, therefore, as your heavenly Father is perfect.
> **Matthew 5:43–48 NIV**

For Your Rivals

Rivals are not enemies, in that, they do not seek to hurt you, but they are in conflict or competition for something you both prize.

Think of athletes on opposite sides, trying to win, with their rival standing in their way, trying to stop them. You may grow to dislike them out of the frustration and the "heat of battle," but the best rivals become friends after the contest or conflict is decided.

Dear God,

This is a hard prayer to pray. When I go to (work/school/etc.) I have nothing but conflict with (name or names). For some reason, we always find ourselves on opposite sides of everything, and we end up sniping at each other.

I know this isn't what You want from me, and I know I must handle it better. I do my best to behave in a way that would please You, but I often fall short.

I am sorry for any bitterness I bring to this conflict, and I pray we can develop a degree of peaceful coexistence if actual friendship is not possible.

This prayer, though, is specifically for (name or names). I ask Your blessings on their life and allow them to have success in proportion to their talents. May they be happy and fulfilled in their life outside, as well as here at (work/school/etc.).

I also pray they receive the insight that for most of us, we win some and lose some. Since that is true, we need to enjoy the wins and turn the page on the losses without lashing out or sabotaging other people.

Thank You for working on my life and theirs to make us both better people.

In Jesus' name, I pray, Amen!

For Enemies

In contrast to rivals, who just happen to be in your way as you compete for a job, a romantic interest, a city basketball championship, or class valedictorian, enemies often oppose you for who you are, not because you stand in their way. They aren't competing with you. They dislike you. You may feel the same about them and act in a similar fashion.

Your ultimate enemy is Satan, who only wants to capture your soul through sin and a forsaking of the Lord. He means to ruin you by any means necessary so that you can spend eternity away from God, in a place of eternal torment.

Your earthly enemies may work for Satan, but they may also be reacting to some other stimulus, whether it's some bias (racism, sexism, or a family feud), a misunderstanding (they think you did something to hurt them even if you're innocent), or some other matter. Satan may be working on them and you at the same time.

It's this last possibility, I believe, that makes praying for your enemy imperative. It probably isn't their fault. Through some combination of factors, they and you have been pitted against each other. Satan may be manipulating you and your "enemy." That's even more reason to stay close to Jesus, who always scares the devil away.

Dear God,
I pray today for someone I consider an enemy
(person's name).

As you know, we have never gotten along. Perhaps it has to do with (some incident or conflict in the past), or it may just be something that sets them off about me. For my part, they dislike me so much that I feel almost obliged to dislike them as much.

Lord, I pray for (person's name). Bless them with peace and calm. Show them I mean them no harm. Help them to soften their heart, realizing they and I were made by the same loving God, and we are children of that God.

Ideally, we could become good friends, even laughing about our former mutual disdain. But even if we can't, let us coexist peacefully without the tension and unnecessary antipathy.

Lord, thank You for this opportunity to grow closer to You by learning how to better deal with those who dislike or wish me ill. I know this makes me more like Jesus, a goal You and I both share.

Thank You for resolving this difficult issue for me and (name of the soon-to-be-former enemy)

In Jesus' name, I pray, AMEN!

For Criminals

Whether newly accused or finally convicted, criminals or alleged criminals are not usually sympathetic figures.

This is especially true if their crime has affected you personally (as a victim yourself or someone close to you).

Realize that despite their wrongdoing (if they are guilty), they were created in the image of God and by God to love and to be loved by. This doesn't exempt them from accountability here on earth, but we should pray they take full advantage of God's grace and mercy. God loves them too, despite their sins, just as He loves you.

Dear Lord,
It is so hard to pray this prayer!

Thank You for hearing me and understanding my hesitation.

As You know, (I, or someone I love) was the victim of (name of crime) and suffered (injury, illness, death, violent attack, loss of money, property, reputation, sense of safety, etc.). The person(s) who did this (has/have been captured and are awaiting trial or are still at large).

Lord, help me to trust that law enforcement and the legal systems will do their jobs well, capturing this criminal, getting the right person, trying their case in court, and delivering a guilty verdict and appropriate punishment for what they did.

Having said that, I pray for the soul of this person/these people. Though they have done evil and caused great pain and suffering, I know You created them and love them. I know You want to see them repent and accept You as their Lord and Savior.

Because that is what You want, it is also what I want. I ask You to intervene with them and help them see the error of their ways. Help them to get the help they need to reform their lives and live as You intended us to when You created us.

Thank You, dear God, for helping me learn mercy and forgiveness through this awful incident. I am grateful for the mercy You show me, which is the blueprint for all mercy, everywhere.

In the restoring name of Jesus, I pray, AMEN!

For People Who Have Hurt Me or Someone Close to Me

People who have hurt others intentionally range from a kid cheating at kickball to teasing or demeaning someone to bullying, any type of abuse, harassment, and crimes like assault, rape, murder, arson, and more.

These things are difficult to forgive, and they get harder the more serious they are.

Jesus calls us to forgive as the Lord has forgiven us. Since instant forgiveness is often awfully hard, we should pray for ourselves to get there, but also for the person who did the deed.

For the Victim

Dear Lord,
As You know, I was (bullied, abused, or mistreated) OR I was the victim of an (assault, robbery, etc.) This incident has marked me for a long time, and I am having trouble getting over it.

Lord, I have sometimes prayed for the person(s) who did this to suffer and be hurt because of what they did. I know You don't work that way, but I am still very angry.

I ask You, please help me remove the bitterness and anger from my heart. It is not helping me, and it is certainly not doing anything to punish or convict the person(s) who did this.

Lord, I ask You to soften my heart and forgive, even if they don't apologize, or even if they don't care at all.

This is the first step for me toward healing from this, and I ask this in the healing name of Jesus, AMEN.

For the Perpetrator

Dear Lord,
As you know, I was victimized by (name), who hurt me very badly, and I am still suffering from the hurt I endured. I have prayed to You a lot for the heart to forgive, and I am grateful for You helping me move forward to do that.

One thing I have not done is to pray for the person who hurt me. Having had some time to reflect, I don't imagine people "plan" to be the way this person is and to hurt others in this way. Something or someone hurt them, and it set in motion the events that resulted in my being hurt.

For that reason, I pray for their healing and recovery from their hurts, and part of that recovery is never to do that again and to make amends to the people whom they have already victimized.

In the gracious name of Jesus, I pray, AMEN!

For Victims of Calamity or Wrongdoing
The term "victim" is extremely broad.

A person can be a victim of a crime. The crime may be minor, e.g., someone at the office took my lunch and ate it. Or it could be a serious crime, including assault, rape, armed robbery, kidnapping, arson, or even murder.

A person or group can be a victim of an accident. The accident may be minor, e.g., someone closes a car door on their hand. Or it could be one of a whole range of more serious accidents, including industrial explosions, car crashes, slips, and falls, boating accidents, and plane crashes.

A whole population can even be victims together of a natural disaster like a hurricane, tornado, wildfire, flood, or blizzard.

And, of course, victims of any of the above might be alive or dead. If they are alive, you might look at the section on praying for those who are sick or injured. If they are deceased, you might look at the section on praying for someone grieving.

The possible combinations of details related to how someone might be a victim are many, and this section is only to give some ideas, which will focus on the broadest and most common types of victimhood.

For Victims of Natural Disasters

Dear God,
Bless and protect the people who live and work in (Name the area where the storm is likely to hit).

Hopefully, they have taken steps to ensure their safety and are inside where it is hopefully safe and dry. Protect them and their property from ruin, and let aid arrive quickly if there is significant damage.

Lord, as the region recovers and rebuilds, let the good in people eclipse the bad and let neighbors show kindness and mercy to one another and help one another out. Let those who come to help not take advantage of the victims who may be desperate.

Lord, we know these natural upheavals are part of living in a broken world. We recognize that a certain amount of this is necessary and that living in certain places involves some degree of risk. We ask You to bless those in the path of the storm with safety, whether it means staying inside or in the basement or leaving to shelter somewhere safe.

We thank You, Lord, that every storm moves on, and though there is much to clean up and/or rebuild, the sun comes out, and life begins again.

In Jesus' name, I pray, Amen!

For Victims of Gun Violence

Lord, as part of the evil that runs through this broken world, Satan created war. War necessitated weapons, and eventually, the gun was invented. It has evolved into an increasingly effective killing machine, easily portable, and thus, available to use if you lose your temper or sense danger.

Fear, vengeance, and hatred are the root causes of violence, and guns are often the tool Satan uses to exact the maximum amount of pain to the most people with the least effort.

Whether in the cities, the suburbs, or out in the country, gun violence happens everywhere. The trauma echoes far beyond the pistol smoke through the victims, their families, their communities, and often including the perpetrator.

Lord, I ask for healing for anyone who has been shot and was not killed. I ask for them to be able to move past the trauma, fear, pain, anger, and lust for revenge that accompanies this.

Let their families, friends, teachers, and coworkers support the victims in their healing, both physically and mentally, so that they do not seek revenge or act out in other destructive ways.

For those who have died, let them rest in peace, whether they were the intended victim or not. Bless their families and friends with happy memories of those who were lost, whether they were innocent bystanders or they were at fault for the violence.

Bless those with calmer heads to prevail over the anger, blaming, excuse-making, and thirst for vengeance.

In Jesus' loving name, Amen!

For Victims of Bullying

Dear God,
The best time in many of our lives is our youth. Before the responsibilities of adulthood, we are increasingly free from parental control and can start to make our own decisions. How we do with that depends on how well we have been prepared for dealing in the wider world.

For children and teenagers who are bullied— verbally and physically abused by others— youth is painful, fearful, and unmanageable at times. And in today's world, with the ability to load cell phone pictures and videos onto Facebook, Twitter, and Instagram, this abuse is not confined to school or anyplace else. Bullies need not even leave home to inflict emotional distress.

Lord, I ask Your protection for the victims of bullying. I ask for others to step up and insist that the abuse stop, whether they are teachers, older students, administrators, or coaches.

These kids suffer so much, and they are hemmed in against normal means of responding, including telling teachers and others or even avoiding the tormentor in the first place.

When hemmed in, people who see no way out of their agony think of solutions, and they sometimes choose to try suicide. A tragic and unnecessary end because the bullies could have decided to leave them alone. Please prevail on these desperate kids to hold on and not end their lives.

Bless these poor kids with positive reinforcement, including from peers who like them and are not afraid of the bullies. Bless them with good advice from parents, teachers, and older students who may have been through something similar in their lives.

Finally, bless the bullies, especially younger kids who don't know how to act. Let them be blessed with positive examples and be punished appropriately for their bad behavior.

If the bullies are also victims of abuse, as they sometimes are, let their abusers seek help, change their behaviors, or be removed from where they can cause harm.

Lord, this problem cries out for Your help. So many innocents are living miserable lives because of other people getting a kick out of abuse.

Thank You for prevailing, as You always do, to help the less fortunate, the abused, and the marginalized.

Thank You for loving us all and for working in our lives to make things better.

In Jesus' almighty name, I pray, AMEN!

For Victims of Domestic Violence

Dear Lord,
In our broken world, we have frustrations, problems, and setbacks. We have difficult relationships with family, friends, coworkers, teammates, classmates, and even strangers.

Many of us are blessed to live in committed relationships, promising to love each other, and being a couple.

Sometimes the frustrations outside, which we are often encouraged to bury and not talk about, explode at home on the ones we love the most, who will not leave us and of whom we take undue advantage.

Sometimes it is verbal or psychological abuse, demeaning the other person in ways that serve only to hurt and debase.

Other times it is violent, with one partner physically threatening, beating, or sexually abusing the other. Once this starts, it seldom stops without either an intervention (usually by law enforcement), separation (the abuser or the abused leave and don't return), serious injury, or death.

Lord, none of these outcomes is acceptable if the abuse continues. Thank You for Your guidance when You preached love and tenderness, even laying out in Scripture the right behavior for husbands and wives. Unfortunately, we sometimes resort to violence instead.

Lord, bless and heal those who are abused, whether physically or verbally. Let them escape from danger. Let others believe them when they tell.

Let there be restrictions to keep the abuser and their victims separate while the abuser gets help. If they don't get help, the relationship should end.

Also, bless the abusers, who did not grow up dreaming of being an abuser. Help them get support to understand and then change their behavior, so they can resume their relationships, dealing with their frustrations and anger appropriately, and never through violence and abuse.

I ask all this, in Jesus' name, Amen!

For Those in Authority

We often forget to pray for our leaders, whether in school, at work, in law enforcement, the military, in church, or all levels of government.

It's important to remember that behind the teacher's room door, in the patrol car, on the battlefield, in the pulpit, or in the seats of government power, these leaders are people. And as people with authority to protect us and the duty to carry it out successfully, they deserve our prayers too.

Leaders come under a lot of pressure. For one thing, any decision they make will upset someone. It's rare that a course of action is both clear and universally accepted. There is a degree of jealousy toward the leader for some, who feel they are equal to or better qualified than the leader to fill the position. Some peers may be competitors. There are a lot of moving parts.

Leaders are also expected to have the right answers and right actions to deal with a crisis, manage the spending of their organization, and manage relationships with employees, unions, voters/constituents, boards of directors, their local and national community and government agencies and organizations, and regulatory rules and regulations. Not to mention internal competition within the organization and the competition from those who want what the leader and his organization already have.

Maybe your leader is not very effective. Maybe they are:

- A manager who is a dictator, micromanager, or narcissist

- A politician you didn't vote for and don't agree with

- A police officer who arrests a member of your family

- A pastor who is awkward or introverted making them seem aloof

- A platoon leader who you are afraid may endanger the lives of you and your colleagues.

Here are some ideas for praying on behalf of leaders:

For Elected Officials

Those who we elect to make our laws and represent us in the government are responsible for helping to maintain a free society that works the way we want it to work. Quite often, we disagree with them on one, many, or all issues. Despite this, and the regular cycle of election and reelection campaigns, we all lose when our elected officials fail. For this reason and that they are human beings, created by God to love and be loved like we were, we should pray for their success in carrying out their duties.

Dear Lord,
Our country is a wonderfully free, diverse, fascinating place.

You have blessed us with an endless variety of lands, climates, cultures, and peoples from all over the world. Our elected officials are in place to help manage the ongoing affairs of our country so that the great things are safeguarded, and those areas where we struggle can get better.

Though we disagree on some issues, it's in everyone's best interest to pray for our elected officials to do a good, moral, and ethical job in their position. Bless our leaders with good conscience and the courage to stand for the right thing, especially in the face of vocal and passionate opposition.

I pray that these folks remember who they represent, and they will do what is right for most people. Let their service be pure, and their integrity be unquestionable.

We ask this in Jesus' name, AMEN!

For Law Enforcement Officers

Lord, thank You for the wonderful land in which we live. We are grateful for the many opportunities to live, love, and thrive in the freedom with which You have blessed us.

Lord, as You know, we need people to keep the peace, ensuring laws are followed so that we are all safe and can enjoy this freedom.

This dangerous work requires much training and expertise, but it also requires a level of bravery and selfless commitment to duty that isn't present in everyone.

Thank You for blessing us with people willing to protect us and our loved ones by doing this work. Always watch over them and protect them from the evils they are out there to stop. Let them do their work with consistent integrity and more judgment as they deal with difficult situations and people all day long.

Thank You for the blessings of law and order so that our lives can be happier and less stressful than they might otherwise be.

In Jesus' holy name, I pray, AMEN!

For Members of the Armed Forces

Dear God,

Thank You for our beautiful country and for the freedom with which You have blessed us.

It has been the case for so long that we might be inclined to take it for granted.

Fortunately, we do not do that, and while our country has enemies in the world, we have the men and women of the armed forces whose role is to protect our way of life from those who would disrupt it.

I ask Your blessing on all our service members around the world. Thank You for their willingness to sacrifice their time and safety for our benefit back home. Protect them from the enemy and their weapons. Protect them from accidents and other mishaps. Always guard their health and safety.

Let us also remember their families and friends who worry about them when they are in harm's way. Bless them with faith that their loved ones return safe and healthy to a grateful nation.

In Jesus' name, we pray, AMEN!

For Leaders Managing a Crisis

Dear God,
Please bless, protect, and support (person or group) who is/are dealing with (crisis type).

At times like this, when the future is uncertain, we support our leaders and pray for their success in managing the situation to minimize loss of life, property, jobs, money, or any other precious resource.

Bless all those involved, including the people affected and the peoples whose job it is to resolve/manage/mitigate this situation.

Thank You, Lord, for always being with us, protecting, and serving us as no one else can.

Thank You for Your mercy and Your help in all things.

In Jesus' name, I pray, AMEN!

For Those in Leadership Positions in Organizations

Dear God,
Bless our (company, church, government, military) leader(s).

Lord, help me remember that behind every official role from manager trainee to insurance company vice president, newly minted police officer, a field commander leading his first platoon, or even President of the United States is a human being.

We may not always agree with what those in authority decide to do, including actions, priorities, and many, many decisions made every day. The reality is these are the people in the roles right now. And their success can lead to our success, safety, spiritual growth, societal peace, and prosperity, and, in some cases, our survival.

They are also people who have similar problems, worries, distractions, and relationships (personal and professional) as the rest of us. They are worthy of our love, as Christ preached it to truly hope they succeed in doing good while doing well. That they do their work the right way, as Jesus would do.

So I pray for the success of (name of role, organization, or individual leaders). We know their success should enable us to pursue our lives in safety, peace, and education. We also recognize that many of us would be unwilling or unable to perform these jobs and that, in the best case, they are performing a vital function.

Bless them with wisdom to minimize risks and take advantage of opportunities that will benefit the organization and the people they serve. Help them avoid the sins of corruption, as well as the other sins that affect all of us.

Thank You for providing these folks to help in ways large and small, manage and control our daily lives.

Your prayer routine will definitely include praying for people. We learn from an early age to pray for our parents, grandparents, siblings, aunts, uncles, and even pets. Many of us don't pray for anything or anyone else.

Remember as much as possible to pray for those who are less fortunate as well as those toward whom society tends to turn a cold shoulder. Despite their deeds, they are also created in the image of God. Of all the ways we can grow spiritually, one that impresses God more than most is when we develop the ability to pray for our enemies.

Doing this helps the person or persons for whom you pray. But it may help you even more.

Appendix 4 – Prayers for Things

As we said, there are untold millions of possible "things" for which we can pray.

And we know God is more about need than about want, but He will deliver on a want of yours as often as He chooses. It may be your want will help deliver someone else's need, but whatever the reason, you will always get what you truly need and sometimes what you want. Sometimes, they are the same thing.

Below are some suggestions of how you can pray to God for something or other that you want and may also need. Keeping in mind all your prayer fundamentals (see Part II), you delve in.

Don't worry; He already knows what you're going to ask for, and He is pleased to hear from you on the matter.

Patience and Mercy

How often do we need patience and mercy?

All day, every day. We need patience with waiting, patience with spouses and kids, patience with strangers in traffic, or patience for waiting in line behind those unruly strangers.

We also need patience as we wait for God. We know He can do anything, and He can do it right this minute. Why wouldn't He? Because He wants you to learn patience. He wants you to trust Him.

Dear God,

Thank You for hearing me and helping me through this hectic day. I felt like I was in a hurry from the time I left the house until I closed my eyes to sleep tonight.

Lord, one byproduct of my rushing around, is that I become extremely impatient with people who walk, drive, act, or react too slowly.

Or they don't share my sense of urgency.

Or they are not as skilled and efficient as I would like them to be.

Or they don't remember things I told them already.

Or they just don't understand me.

Help me remember, Lord, that I am not the only one with things to do. Help me remember that not everyone shares my urgency, which sometimes may be unnecessary. Help me know I don't know everything and that, contrary to popular belief, this customer is not always right.

Lord, people make mistakes and do things that mess me up. Help me to be merciful to these people, realizing I do things that mess other people up. I don't mean to; I'm just human. Remind me they don't mean to either.

Help me not to judge people for their failings. Someone who seems clueless may have a personal problem taking their mind elsewhere. Let me have mercy.

Another, who puts the eggs at the bottom of the grocery bag, may have a learning disability, or they're working their first job, or they were not properly trained.

Since I don't know these things, I cannot judge them, yet I try to anyway. Help me stop that. They don't know what I'm going through, and you know I am not perfect either.

Thank You for teaching me mercy and grace by having it with me.

In Jesus' name, I pray, Amen!

Job and Career Matters

Aside from families, or maybe instead of them, our jobs and careers are the aspects of our lives most likely to cause us to rejoice at new opportunities, despair at opportunities missed or lost, and encounter considerable stress, which we then have to manage. Factor in coworkers trying to manage similar, but not identical, baskets of issues, and you can all add both camaraderie and conflict to the menu.

Below are some ideas for praying about your job or career or that of someone else's, whom you care about. You can use them verbatim, substituting details where needed, or use it as a guide, to help you make up your own. It doesn't matter if you pray and thank the Lord for being with you and helping you with all your problems and concerns.

Praying for a Job You Want for Yourself

Dear Lord,
Thank You for hearing my prayer. As You know, I am interested in a new job (name it if you wish) at (my current workplace or a new workplace, named if you wish).

I believe I have the experience and knowledge to be successful in this position, but I know others have the same things.

Lord, I don't know how it will turn out, but I pray I put my best foot forward, make a good presentation of myself and my abilities, and be relaxed and confident. I would love to have this job, but if it is not in the cards this time, let me enhance my reputation here by being a solid, serious candidate.

Your will be done.

In Jesus' name, I pray, AMEN!

Praying for Someone Else to Get a Job

This is also a prayer for a person,

Lord,

I pray today for (name), who, as You know, needs a job as soon as possible. I know they are trying hard, and things haven't worked out yet.

I know You have something planned for them, and I know You will resolve it in Your perfect timing.

In the meantime, let them grow and learn whatever it is You need them to learn. Thank You for faithfully working on all of us, especially (name). It's tough to wait sometimes, and it's even tougher to fail, but I know You will deliver them from this difficult time when the time is right.

Thank you for answering this prayer.

In Jesus' healing name, AMEN!

For Help

Help is another subjective word. One man's help is another man's hindrance.

Still, we define helping as the well-intended involvement of someone to aid in the completion of a task or achievement of a goal of someone else.

We can't always go it alone. Sometimes, when the task is too big, complex, or expansive, it's impossible.

We don't always have someone to help us either. These prayers ask God for the help you need.

I Need Help!

Dear God,
You know better than I do how much help I need and with what. I am struggling with (list, if you wish) so many things, and sorting it all out and fixing it is more than I can handle.

I surrender, Lord. It's too much for me, and I need Your help. I am out of ideas, out of excuses, and out of time. Please, Lord, help me!

I am so grateful for Your hearing my prayer. Thank You for Your help today, yesterday, and tomorrow.

In Jesus' name, I pray, expectantly, AMEN!

Someone Else Needs Help

Lord Jesus, I am praying for (name, if you wish) who is struggling and needs Your help (or list concerns, if you wish).

Lord, send Your healing love and perfect help to them in Your perfect timing and help them resolve this burden, hurting them so much.

In Jesus' name, Amen!

Everyone Needs Help (Prayer for Help Wherever It's Needed)

Lord, in this world, we have trouble, just as You promised.

So many are working on intractable problems, and the frustration of failure and the feeling of being overwhelmed are rampant.

It's comforting to know You are with them and will provide help to them at the perfect time and in the most perfect way.

I ask Your help for all who are downhearted, overwhelmed, or plain tired of failing to do it on their own.

Let them see Your awesome power working for their sake to straighten out what is bent, repair what is hopelessly broken, and soothe the frustrated and defeated minds with Your blessed relief.

Thank You for hearing my prayer and for answering me as You always do. I love You!

In Jesus' mighty name, I pray, AMEN!

Something You Merely Want

As was the case with the Lamborghini, sometimes we just want something, or we think we do.

Here is a shell of a prayer into which you can fit a request for a thing you merely want.

Dear God,

You know I am more than blessed with everything I have, and I want for nothing important. I am interested in getting a (laptop, motorcycle, vacation to Aruba, fishing rod, Xbox 360, kitchen remodel, etc.)

I know this seems like a frivolous request because it is. I am perfectly fine with what I have.

Although I had not planned to use it specifically to solve world hunger, clean our air and water, or end all wars without further bloodshed, I certainly will take that opportunity if it should arise. But really, I'd just like to enjoy a new thing.

If it is not Your will for me to have this, then I won't have it, but it sure is something I'd like to have.

Thank You for hearing my request and caring about what I want as well as what I need. I know that doesn't necessarily equate to a yes, but I appreciate Your consideration and the love that underlies it.

I love You as well.

In Jesus' name, I pray, AMEN!

Appendix 5 – Prayers for Salvation

Any of these simple prayers, when prayed sincerely, will be the most important words you ever say in your life. It is through this heartfelt prayer declaration that you surrender your life to Jesus Christ, your Savior and the Son of God, who made you and who loves you more than anyone else in creation.

These are just some suggestions, but all convey a sense of surrender, an expression of gratitude for God's saving grace, an understanding that His grace and mercy are truly gifts we do not deserve, and love for God and His care for us.

If that is what is truly in your heart, and you pray it, God will know. And your salvation is assured. Congratulations and welcome to His kingdom!

> *Lord,*
> *I have questions and doubts, but to the extent I understand, I know I want You in my life. I want to be saved. I know You don't fear my questions or doubts, and I will get the answers I need. I don't want to put this off anymore. It's too important. Thank You for being patient with me while I procrastinated. In the mighty name of Jesus, AMEN!*
>
> *Lord Jesus, save me! (Note: With the right intention, this will do it! The Lord knows your heart, so your words are secondary.)*

Oh, Lord,
I am realizing how blessed I am and always have been. I realize You are the source of all my blessings, and I have neglected You for a long time. Please, come into my life and change me, make me better, and save me. Thank You, Thank You for loving me despite my sins and mistakes. Show me Your path for my life. In your name, I pray, AMEN!

Lord,
I don't understand it all, but I believe You, and I want you to come into my life. In Jesus' name, I pray, AMEN!

Dear God,
My life feels complicated, and I am not sure what I should do. The one solid thing is that starting a relationship with You will be good for me. I am committed to worshiping You, trusting You, and loving You. Thank You for Your gift of salvation. In Jesus' name, AMEN!

Lord Jesus Christ,
I accept the gifts You have offered me. Thank You for Your sacrifice on the cross to save me from my sinful life. I have many questions and even some doubts, but I will get my answers with You. I'm confident I will grow in faith as I gain knowledge.
In your holy name, I pray, AMEN!

Dear God, I'm In!

(Note: That's the whole prayer, if you feel it in your heart!)

Lord Jesus,
Come into my life in every aspect. Thank You for offering Your salvation, and thank You for helping me accept it. I am sorry for the many sins I have committed, and I thank You for Your grace and patience. Help me grow and develop my faith over the remainder of my life and beyond. Thank you for loving me so much. In your holy name, I pray, AMEN.

Dear God,
I am lost and overwhelmed. My life is chaos, and I have been struggling mightily without progress. Lord, come into my life and help me make sense of it. I surrender control to You, as You know best the changes I need to make.

In your powerful name, I pray, AMEN!

Appendix 6 – Prayers for Forgiveness of Sins

For Sins of Character Failure

Dear God,
I'm sorry for my sin of (describe sin).

I am sorry because I know better. I know it was a sin, and that makes it worse. I didn't think about consequences or You standing beside me. I didn't do anything but follow my temptation.

Lord, this is a terrible weakness of mine, and I need Your help to conquer it. Help me to be stronger and less susceptible to any of the demons that lead me to sin.

Thank You for Your forgiveness. Although I am not deserving of it, You do it because You love me, and that is the best thing I know.

Thank You.
In Jesus' name, I pray, Amen!

Dear God,
When I was younger, and to a lesser extent now, I tended to judge people. Some through reputation, others through appearance, and a few with whom I had direct experience.

While I was not a bully per se, those whom I judged negatively, I did not treat with respect and love, as You have taught.

There were others, whom I did not personally mistreat, but was silent as others did, some of whose names I cannot recall if I ever knew them. I pray for those people because I know how deep the scars of these experiences in our youth cut. I pray that if the same situation occurred now, I would show more courage and kindness than I did then.

I offer this repentance in Jesus' name, AMEN!

For Sins of Disobedience

Dear God,
I know I must return to church.

I know there are people there You want me to meet. I realize that being around other believers will grow my faith and help me uncover my purpose.

I know I could have done this many times already and chose not to. I realize this is either disobedience, or it could be that I should not return to the same church. I don't know.

I know I am thinking about church the same way I think about being with friends or being social. I overthink the awkwardness, the potential for discomfort or being offended, then dismiss the whole enterprise as too hard.

Then I waste time watching TV or playing with my phone and pointedly avoiding the problem.

Thank You for forgiving me of this serious sin, as I know worshiping in fellowship is one of my duties as a believer.

Thank You for Your help in letting me resolve it.

I am sorry for these sins and will work hard not to do so in the future.

In Jesus' name, Amen!

Dear Lord,
I am sorry for my sins, especially including the judgment of others, inconsistency of character, and procrastination on my duties, small and large.

Forgive me of all these and the many others I commit, whether intentionally or not. I am grateful You make the old things new, and the bad disappear in the light of Your power and glory. Show me the better way, and give me the strength to follow, as it may not be easy, but it is surely right.

In Jesus' name, I pray, AMEN!

Dear Jesus,

I am sorry for all the times I have failed to follow Your direction, which I realize is sometimes through willful disobedience, although other times it is through misunderstanding or laziness.

Help me to fight off willful disobedience, which I can if I stay close to You, and help me grow in my understanding of Your will so that my misunderstandings are few. Help me fight my tendency to rest too much, waste time, and other lazy, unproductive habits that reduce my effectiveness.

I am sorry for my sins, and I will work to reduce them as much as I can.

In Your name, I pray, AMEN!

Dear Lord,

Help me avoid casualness and the sometimes accompanying disrespect and irreverence for Your power and majesty.

Help me to remember I am a sinner, and my only road to salvation is through You. I rejoice in the fact that while this is my only chance for salvation, it is readily available to me, and I can learn about it through Your Word.

I am grateful for this opportunity, and I am hopeful I will take full advantage of it. I understand You offer it in unfailing love and care, and I strive to receive it the same way.

In Jesus' name, AMEN!

Dear God,
I am sorry for the failures I have had. I have done some things badly, but most things I have failed at have been through a lack of my persistence. Being on the right track and refusing to follow it is a lack of trust. I am sorry for this sin.

I know You can do all things. I know You won't leave me hanging. I know You won't forget me. But I also know You need me to start, and in my head, I have, but in my heart, I haven't.

I'm not sure what it is, but I know with Your help, I can be more diligent and more successful than I have been in the past.

I ask for this help in Jesus' name, AMEN!

Dear God,
I always feel as though I give things to You only after I have messed them up, trying to figure it out myself. I'm sorry about this.

Even for You, cleaning up unnecessary messes is not how You want to spend Your time.

Lord, I will do better at seeking You first, rather than going it alone and wasting time and energy. Doing things with Your blessing and help makes the result better, and often the work is easier.

Thank You for forgiving me of this sin. I am grateful for Your mercy and grace.

In Jesus' name, I pray, AMEN!

Oh, God,
I am sorry for my disobedience when it comes to money. I know it is why we struggle and that greed is a problem for us. Help me to not only think but also to act in charity in a way that pleases You.

I ask this in Jesus' name, AMEN!

Dear Lord,
I know I am disobedient and fall short in many areas. I am grateful for Your mercy and the salvation from Your Son Jesus, for making my flaws less important than my faith and love for You.

Thank You for Your mercy and blessing on me, a sinner. In Jesus' name, AMEN.

For Sins of Idolatry

Dear Lord,
You know we have made an idol out of money,
comfort, and health care coverage. You know
we don't follow Your directions the way we
should because we don't like what seems like
a risk.

Help us realize that when we follow Your
direction, there is no risk. All things will work
out when they are part of Your plan.

Let us realize we can have a wonderful, joyful,
happy life no matter what happens. You have
brought us through trouble before, and You
always will bring us through the trouble. You
have also provided gifts and blessings we need
to appreciate and be grateful for every single
day.

Lord, I am grateful for Your insights and Your
mercy and forgiveness of sins.

In Jesus' name, I pray, Amen.

For Sins of Impatience and Anger

Dear God,
I am sorry for my impatience.

I know You are working things out, and
everything will fall into place in Your perfect
timing.

Let these difficulties and delays stretch and grow my faith so that I know in my heart as well as in my head that all will be well, thanks to You.

Thank You for helping me get better.

In Jesus' name, AMEN!

Dear Jesus,
I am sorry for my sins, particularly worry and impatience, as they are both unproductive and demonstrate a lack of faith.

Help me grow past these sins, as I believe in Your plan so that my faith continues to mature, and I am able, with your strength, to benefit Your kingdom.

In Your Name, AMEN!

Oh, Lord,
Please forgive my impatience and help me see what I need to do to move forward.

Maybe I'm doing what You want me to do, and I just need to be patient. But if I am missing something—or everything—and need to do things differently, please make it clear enough for me to see.

I know life is temporary on earth, and we are here to do a job for You before we can come home to heaven. Let me do that job as well as I possibly can.

Replace my impatience with faith, worship, and reverence, and make me an example to those around me that I cannot be shaken if You are with me, which is always.

I love You,

In Jesus' name, I pray, expectantly, AMEN!

For the Sin of Lust

Dear Lord,
I am sorry I am a lustful person.

Lord, when I look back, I feel ashamed for how I have thought and acted. I was so driven by lust and so totally absent from you (though you were there with me), I could do little.

I have so much growing up to do!

Now, I realize that, though I have grown up some, I still have so far to go. There is still so much wisdom that eludes me. I am still fooled by the enemy's nonsense. I am still sinful in so many ways.

Lord, help me to repent my lustful thoughts and show the self-control that is a gift of your Holy Spirit.

Remind me that I am not alone, and I should want to impress You with my behavior, not act or think like a fool.

Thank You for Your mercy and commitment to shaping me for eternal life with You. That is the greatest gift of all.

In Your name, I pray, AMEN!

For the Sin of Not Taking Proper Care of Myself

Many of us let ourselves go as we age. This is a combination of being busy (working, raising kids, etc.) and taking for granted that our strength, vitality, health, and stamina from our youth will not desert us when we get older.

Sometimes the first inkling we have that this is not true is a heart attack or some other catastrophic medical event. Other times it's playing pickup basketball after a long time away and being stunned that you can no longer run, jump, or play like you used to.

Realizing our bodies, like everything else we have, are gifts from God may help us move self-care higher on our priority list. So might the aforementioned medical event or the realization you just don't feel good much of the time.

For Christians, we know when we accepted Christ, the Holy Spirit came to live in us, providing guidance and encouragement as we grow in the faith. Caring for where God lives on earth—in each of us—makes failing to care for your body a sin you should repent and commit to changing.

Dear God,

You give us these bodies to use while we're here on earth. Some take care of them, making them as healthy and fit as they can. They exercise, eat intelligently, sleep enough, and manage their stress.

By contrast, I am almost completely inactive. I am eating poorly, making bad decisions, and allowing depression to take hold again. I have completely wasted the investments I made in myself, losing weight, and starting to feel and even look better.

Now I am gaining weight again, have completely undermined my organization system, and am in my current state of being overwhelmed and unable to act on anything.

My back hurts, my head hurts, and my neck hurts. I am afraid this is what aging is. I have few contacts outside my family, hate my job, and lack passion or even persistent interest in anything.

It's becoming difficult to determine whether I am unhealthy because I am unhappy or if I am unhappy because I'm unhealthy. I guess it doesn't matter since it's obvious I am both, and caring for my body has to be a big key toward resolving both problems.

Lord, as is becoming a theme with me, I have tried to solve these problems without You. Though I tend to default to not wanting to ask anyone for help, I know I must shake that feeling when it comes to getting help from You. You are the only one who will always help me, and You can fix anything that needs to be fixed.

Lord, I ask You, please, help me to take better care of myself. Whatever you see as my priority, please point me in that direction. I know Your plan is better than mine, and I want to follow and obey you in all things.

Thank You for caring about me and helping me get better.

In Jesus' name, I pray, AMEN!

For Sins Committed In Parenting

For Faith, Though Children Are Grown

Dear God,
I feel bad I was a poor faith role model when my kids were younger. I was impatient, irritable, lazy, and openly negative about the church. While we had them go through religious education and the sacraments of the Catholic Church, we did it out of duty, not faith, and rarely with joy.

I regret not being committed to their spiritual growth, but I hadn't grown my spirit very much either. I feel strongly that had I accepted and trusted You with my whole heart when I was their age, I would have saved myself much pain and stress.

I realize I was not who I am now, a committed believer in You through Your Son, Jesus Christ. A child of God—worthy through Your Son to be an heir in Your Kingdom.

Help me remember this is part of Your plan, and I am who I am now, and they are who they are, and Your will, in the end, will be done.

If it is Your will, help me to succeed in bringing my children to You so that they might find the peace and joy I have and avoid some pain and stress too, and they would, ultimately, be saved. I know You can help me make that happen.

Thank You for giving me such wonderful children and such a great wife to help raise them. Thank You for being with them, as You were with me, during my rebellious years, and for Your patience with them as You had with me.

In Jesus' name, I pray, AMEN!

For Faith, Children Still Young

Dear Lord,
Thank You for the gift and challenge of raising my children. Thank You for (spouse), who is a great help in caring for them every day.

Lord, I struggle to raise them in faith and hope. Although we attend church services, we don't live our faith the way I would like. I am concerned this may affect my children's faith as they grow up.

Lord, let me be a role model of a godly person for my family. Let me show them the right way to be, especially as it relates to You. Let me help them understand You are with them and will help and save them no matter what. Help me share some of Your peace and joy with them.

In Jesus' name, I pray, AMEN!

On the Struggles of Children

Dear God,
You know, (my child) is struggling with a variety of problems. While this is part of growing up, and I have faith it will all be fine, now they are miserable, and as a result, so is the rest of the family.

I remember being that age and how overwhelming everything was and is. Help me be gentle and caring about their concerns and able to give wise, godly counsel that will be clear, helpful, and encouraging. Help us to retain our lines of communication so that we are not cut off from one another so that we're always able to talk.

Help me to be alert to the needs of my children, helping them to grow and mature and to come closer to You in faith and love.

Thank You for the awesome responsibility and guidance You have given me with my wonderful children.

In Jesus' name, I pray, AMEN!

For the Sin of Pride

Pride is a type of idolatry that focuses on yourself. You have a certain image or perception of yourself, which you may have worked hard to craft. And once you have it, you work even harder to maintain it.

Like other things in this list that are not sins in and of themselves, so goes pride. In a sinful sense, pride that leads to conceit and arrogance, which can lead to treating other people badly, is the problem we need to solve.

The seeds of this problem may stretch back to childhood when one's self-perception was just forming. For that reason, pride is a hard sin to overcome.

The first step, and not the only one, is to humble yourself to the One who made you and knows exactly how good you are. You are His child, and He loves you. He will forgive you for your pride and will help you behave in a more humble, thankful, blessed manner.

Dear Lord,
For some time, I have been proud of the fact I am humble. An oxymoronic comment if there ever was one!

The realization that true humility doesn't take pride was my epiphany for yesterday.

Help me be more humble. Let me just BE humble and not think so much about how wonderful I am because of it.

I realize I am fighting myself when I do that, and I also realize it is the enemy undermining what should be a virtue.

Thank You for this revelation and the strength to grow because of it.

Thank You for helping me grow.

In Jesus' name, I pray, AMEN!

Dear Lord,
Growing up, and particularly around sports, there is a lot of talk about pride as a virtue. To be proud of your team, your school, your town, or your country was a good thing.

To take pride in your appearance, the cleanliness of your desk or workspace, or your home and how it looks were framed as being responsible, professional, and mature.

But Lord, while those things are good, there is another type of pride I struggle with. I have trouble admitting when I am wrong or that I don't know something. For some reason, I think I need to have all the answers, even when I have no idea.

I like to be an expert and an authority. I like to be respected for my knowledge and skill. Unfortunately, I like it too much, and at times, it becomes a kind of idol to me. Something I depend on instead of You.

I am sorry for this. It's a recent recognition, and I came to it very slowly over time. Help me to put this preference in its place and not be over-impressed with myself or my expertise.

I will be aware of it and will work hard not to do this anymore. I'm sorry for my sinful pride.

In Your name, I pray for forgiveness.

I love You, AMEN!

For the Sin of Self-Pity

We all feel sorry for ourselves at times. Usually, we are overwhelmed and see no one around who either recognizes it or offers any help. We feel alone, put-upon, and angry (but with no one to yell at).

This tendency to look at ourselves as victims is probably accurate at times. Sometimes others take us for granted and don't appreciate us, or they disrespect and malign us in a way we cannot combat.

From a prayer perspective, you need to separate what may be legitimately happening to you (the taking for granted, et al.) from your feelings about it (the self-pity)

Pray to the Lord as you would pray to Him on behalf of a person — yourself — who is struggling and overwhelmed by some burden or other.

As to the self-pity, pray for relief from that too. Acknowledge how blessed you are. Think about all the things you thank God for, as it is everything and everyone in your life.

Remember, others are worse off than you are on their best day.

Realize you have options, a variety of actions you can choose to address the feeling. Some of those actions will not seem feasible to you, but one or two or a combination of options does the trick.

The key is to admit to the Lord that you are guilty of self-pity despite all you have and the amazing path you are on in life. A few ways of doing this are below:

> Lord,
> I am sorry I let myself get so down and discouraged. I find I am so interested in being by myself that I can't function. Or I don't function might be a better way to describe it.
>
> Help me choose to function well and to interact with people kindly and selflessly. Help me overcome my inadequacies and failings and be successful in whatever You want me to do.

Help me support the people around me by being encouraging and loving in all situations and circumstances.

In Jesus' name, AMEN!

Dear Lord,
I have been struggling with what is popularly known as low self-esteem. I don't like myself much and don't want to expose myself to others who will see me as I see myself.

I am insecure, which makes no sense since I am Your child, and as such, I am more than sufficient. But I still hide and avoid and miss opportunities I would have if I were engaged.

I know self-pity is wrong since I am so blessed, and it is borne of a lie from the enemy, who likes nothing better than to see Your children suffering. But I know I will defeat him with Your help.

In the meantime, I know I am forgoing opportunities to live, grow, and contribute by being so reticent. Help me to stop feeling like I have no friends and go out and make some. Help me to bury the lie that I am not enough— whatever that means. Remind me that I am your child and, as such, am more than good enough.

Thank You for helping me work on this problem, which is a lifelong one for me. Thank You for Your patience while I grow.

In Jesus' name, I pray, AMEN!

Appendix 7 – Prayers for Wisdom

Dear God,

Thank You for my wonderful family. Thank You for blessing us with peace and prosperity, enabling a good and happy life together.

Today, Lord, I pray for (name of loved one), who is having issues with (describe the detail) and about whom I am concerned. I don't know how to reach them with advice that they won't resent or disregard.

Lord, grant me the wisdom to know what, how, and when to say the right thing so that they can absorb it and apply it to improve their life.

Lord, You know we sometimes take our families for granted, and being a part of them is something special because there is no other family like ours. Membership is limited, and we are in exclusive company.

As such, let us appreciate how special this is and look out for one another. And when one of us needs help, let us be open to giving and receiving it in love and respect, knowing our family members love one another very much.

I ask You for this wisdom to use in my relationships and to demonstrate an aspect of Your love for us, in Jesus' name, AMEN!

For Help in Mediating Disputes

Dear God,

Thank You for my friends, colleagues, teammates, and family. Being part of these groups allows me to be blessed by different perspectives, talents, and abilities, enabling me to realize our uniqueness.

Lord, one thing I tend to find is that I am in the middle of disputes between other members of these groups. Being in the middle means if anyone is going to mediate a dispute, it's the middle person.

My problem is I don't know how to do this wisely. I always take one side or another, leaving me open to charges of bias or favoritism, which erodes others' confidence in me and the decisions I make.

Jesus, help me be a peacemaker, a fair and equitable judge, and a staunch advocate for what is right, whether either side agrees with me or not. In the long run, always advocating the right thing leads to the trust and confidence of others, which is something we all want.

Lord, bless me with the wisdom to know when and how to get involved, avoiding situations where my contribution would not lead to a better outcome.

Thank You for hearing me and granting me the wisdom I so sorely need. In Jesus' name, I pray, AMEN!

For the Wisdom to Stay Out of It

Dear Lord,
I sometimes struggle with wanting to fix everything, especially with my family and my closest friends. I tend to rush in and try to tell them what the right answer is, so they can move on and so I can be the hero.

Lord, give me the wisdom to know when I cannot make a positive difference so that while I always hope and pray for a solution, I don't always assume I am the one who has it. I've had trouble learning this, and the result is usually making a bad situation worse, or at least, no better.

Thank You for this insight and for the wisdom to avoid this problem going forward. In Jesus' name, I pray, AMEN!

For the Wisdom to Think, Act, and Communicate Confidently

Heavenly Father,
You know there are times when I doubt myself, leading me to not share my thoughts, which turn out later to be good, accurate, useful, or whatever else. I kick myself for not speaking up.

Lord, help me be a problem solver, an analytical thinker, and a results-oriented person. And as important, let me be confident in the skills and knowledge You've given me so that I might share my ideas in a positive, persuasive way.

Help me to avoid muzzling myself when there is work to be done and ideas are needed. Let me develop the confidence to keep at it and grow as a problem solver in my family, business, church, and social interactions.

Lord, thank You for hearing my prayers and forever working to refine me into the image of Your Son. I have a very long way to go, but Your skilled and faithful work to perfect me is also much appreciated.

In Jesus' name, Amen

Appendix 8 – Prayers for Spiritual Growth

Remember, when you pray for spiritual growth, you know you agree with the Lord, who wants to grow and develop your character and soul for eternity. So you know He will give generously to any growth request you have, in His perfect timing (which may not be immediate).

If you don't pray with expectancy for other things, you can be sure you can expect to receive what you pray for in terms of spiritual growth. God wants it. You want it. And face it, if you didn't want it, and God did, whose will do you think would be done. (Hint – not yours!)

Dear God,
Thank You for creating me as a unique person with unique strengths and areas for growth. Thank You for tirelessly working to shape and refine me, removing my rough edges, polishing my weak areas, and redoubling my strengths.

Lord, help me gain the wisdom to understand Your plan better and better. Help me to be obedient and faithful in working with You to continue Your work in me. Always help me to be more alert to Your presence and help in all things in my life. Thank You for loving me before I knew You. Help me see more clearly how You were carrying me in those years before I got to know You.

Lord, thank You for the peace and joy of knowing I am with You, and You will never, ever fail to keep Your promises. Thank You for saving me, loving me, and wanting me with You in heaven forever.

I love You very much.

In Jesus' name, I pray, AMEN!

Appendix 9 – A Common Question

"If God already knows everything, why does He need my prayer before He'll do anything?"

You're right. God does know everything. But He isn't waiting for you to ask for help. He's already on it. And He is already working on the situation because He already knows about it.

He may be approaching it with different priorities than yours or the person you are praying for. But He is working on the situation.

Because He knows everything, God does not need you to tell Him about a problem in prayer. So why do it?

Because when you pray to God for another person, you are helping at two levels:

- **First,** you are interceding on behalf of a person in need, with the ultimate authority and power over all things, a behavior that always makes God smile because it is an act of love and faith.

- **Second,** God remembers when you take the time to speak to Him on behalf of another person. He does not forget your faith, trust, and love, both for Him and for the person or people you pray for. He loves it when you call on Him for any reason.

God is perfectly capable of running things without your information. But unlike how we might respond to someone distracting us with information we already know while we are working (Picture a persistent backseat driver), God loves a chorus of prayers on behalf of someone who needs them.

Yes, He knows all about the matter at hand, and yes, He understands it from every side, and by the time we even know about it, He has already decided how to move forward.

Keep in mind what God is doing: He is preparing us for eternal life through the continual refinement of our faith and the building of our character. That's not just today, or this week, or this season of life, or even this whole, earthly life, but for our eternal life in heaven with Him.

The answer in the face of life's challenges is always to depend on Him in matters large and small and to obey Him in all situations. Besides this being a pillar of our faith, it's also very practical advice. Trusting the Lord, no matter what happens, is a way to show you love Him.

As a practical matter, trusting the Lord works a lot better than hoping for one of an array of our homegrown solutions doing the trick. When the problem is simple; for example, my shoelace is untied, I can handle that myself. Right? (See Chapter 11 if you missed it!)

Appendix 10 – A Common Lament: "I used to have faith, but I lost it."

Some Reasons People Lose Faith

Sadly, a lot of believers find themselves saying this at some low point in their lives. These low points are tests from God, and due to unstable faith, some believers fail the test.

Sometimes it's a single incident, while other times, it's an accumulation. And because of the intensity of the hurt, they can be difficult to reach with consolation or a reinvigoration for faith in God and His many blessings.

Loss – Loss of something precious. Most common is the loss of a loved one. There is a lady who was a strong believer but who now is not because her son was killed in an automobile accident some years ago. She cannot forgive God for taking her son.

Loss happens in life, and in their minds, everyone knows that. But we have a certain sequence that we have in mind as to these anticipated losses. We expect loss to be of elders, whose long, productive lives have ended, and they are returning to heaven. It hurts, but we don't blame God.

However, sometimes a younger person dies, and there seems to be no good reason. Whether an illness, an accident, violence, war, or something else, these seem to be unnecessary, and some get angry with God. It seems like a broken trust, a broken promise.

Disappointment – Disappointment in something that was supposed to change your life. A broken marriage or engagement, failure to obtain a big promotion, inability to have children, are some of these.

God uses these tests as well, and failing means falling away from Him, not realizing who He is, how He works, or how He sets you up for something better than you can imagine. Passing this test, however, means trusting God. Not just hoping He will deliver you to something better, but knowing in your heart that this disappointment is not the end, it's just a door.

There is a man, a former believer, whose whole identity was tied up in his career. His position in business defined his social circles, his family life, where he lived, what he drove, what he read, for whom he voted… Everything in his life he did because of the executive position he held.

During a downturn with his large company, he was let go. Laid off. Fired. During one thirty-minute meeting with the human resources rep, his entire basis for knowing himself was wiped out. Twenty years of faithful service, erased.

Fear – Fear is really a lack of faith. A belief instead that the evil is going to overcome the good, resulting in injury or ruin to oneself or a loved one.

Fear causes us to close down, board up the windows, sandbag the foundation, and wait because you never know when a storm might come. If it does, we'll be ready.

Our faith in these instances is in the sandbags and plywood on the windows, neither of which will matter if the storm hits just right. Instead of clinging to God and trusting in His power to save us no matter what happens, we put our trust in structural protections that offer no guarantee of safety.

Hatred – The intense disdain for a person or persons is a faith-killing emotion. It is very hard to hold the love for God in the same heart, which houses a hatred of other people whom He also created.

Hate crowds out reason, compassion, kindness, understanding, patience. When such unreasonableness invades, it is hard for faith to endure. Since God doesn't help you destroy the people you hate, you are on your own. Or so you think.

A mind that battles hate more successfully will ask God to examine their heart and help clean out the hatred that is holding them back. God will help with that prayer and deliver some spiritual growth along with it.

So What Do I Do About It?

To return to faith, we must figure out what the cause of our losing it was.

In my case, I was disappointed (and very angry) at the way the Catholic church responded to the abuse scandal. I was disappointed in people. Human beings who, like me, were born into a broken world, riddled with sin.

The disappointment and anger sprang from the way the clergy had always set themselves apart as special (and better, it was implied). Not perfect, but certainly a cut above us common people. To learn that some were abusers, while others covered up for and enabled them, was too much.

But the core of my faith – my belief in God, and His only begotten son, Jesus Christ were unchanged. The Father, Son, and Holy Spirit remained perfect.

I had some questions about why this had been allowed to go on. I got my answers, and realized that God is in control, even as evil is perpetrated, even amongst 'good' people.

Bypassing organized religion and focusing only on the Bible and my relationship with God, I was able to move forward and I am now stronger in faith than I have ever been.

Importantly, I never blamed those in the Catholic Church who chose to stay. They chose to stay and fight for reform. I applaud them. They use their faith in a different way, and they are making progress. I didn't have the stamina to fight like that, and so I went in another direction.

If you are struggling with faith, do you know why? It bears your consideration, as it is literally a life-altering decision. I understand the reflex to turn your back on "all of it." That was what I was doing for a while.

What was your trigger? If you think about it hard enough, God didn't let you down. Jesus Christ didn't let you down. Chances are good that a flawed human being or a group of them let you down.

By focusing on the good news (the Gospel), and by realizing that God offers salvation for the asking, and He doesn't take it back if you make a mistake, you realize that you, too, are a sinner, in need of grace, salvation, and forgiveness.

It's a burden to carry resentment, disappointment, anger, and all the other emotions that come with a lapse in faith. You owe it to yourself to get it back. And if you want to get it back, you will.

Appendix 11 – The Forgotten Rules of Prayer

By KC Hairston[iii]

1. Ask, don't demand (1 John 5:14)
2. Don't give God a test (Deuteronomy 6:16)
3. Believe in the power of prayer (Mark 11:24)
4. Be humble (2 Chronicles 34:27)
5. Be persistent (Luke 18:1)
6. Be specific (Matthew 6:7–8)
7. Husbands and Wife Rule (1 Peter 3:7)
8. Avoid meaningless repetition (Matthew 6:7)
9. Avoid selfishness—motives matter (James 4:3)
10. Pray for your enemies (Matthew 5:44)
11. Pray continuously (1 Thessalonians 5:17)
12. Be righteous (James 5:16)
13. Don't worry—trust God (Matthew 6:25–27)
14. Give thanks for BOTH good and bad (1 Thessalonians 5:18)
15. Include praise (Psalm 106:1)
16. Be careful what you promise to do in your prayers (Ecclesiastes 5:4–5)
17. Don't pray to anyone but God (Exodus 20:3)
18. Think before you pray (Ecclesiastes 5:2)
19. For additional prayer power, add another person (Matthew 18:19–20)
20. Pray for each other (James 5:16)
21. Some prayers require fasting (Matthew 17:18–21)
22. Forgive others—there should be no anger in prayer (Matthew 5:23–24)

23. Repent — sin can annul the authority of your
    prayer (Psalm 66:18, Isaiah 59:2, John 9:31,
    Proverbs 28:13)
24. Pray for those in authority (1 Timothy 2:1–2)
25. Pray for help in resisting temptation (Luke 22:40)
26. Don't pray so that others may see you praying
    (Matthew 6:5)
27. Pray in the name of Jesus (John 14:13–14)
28. Be patient (Psalm 37:7)

Acknowledgements

I am blessed with great support from so many, starting with my wife, Gina, my son J.P. and my daughter Julianna. They are the reason for everything I do, even now that the kids are grown up.

I also want to thank my brother Mike, whose example of humility, kindness, and acceptance is a model to me and everyone who knows him.

My parents, Jim and Mary Lou, live in heaven now, but while they were here with us, they taught us how to emulate the Lord in our dealings with other people, with kindness, respect, and always recognizing the dignity of others. I miss them every day.

A variety of pastors, priests, and other faith leaders have helped me learn more quickly than I would ever do on my own. Special thanks to Pastor Paul Atwater, Pastor Myra Kinds, and Pastor Rick Warren for providing support, insight and instruction to help me over the hurdles of becoming a true believer.

A special thanks to Pam Lagomarsino of Above the Pages Editing Services the editor who takes my nonsense and makes it coherent. Her guidance and suggestions are uniformly helpful and presented with the lightest touch, preserving my otherwise fragile ego.

To the many family and friends who have expressed support for my writing, thank you. Writing is weird, in that you may sit at your desk and like what you just wrote, but you wonder whether you're just kidding yourself.

That remains entirely possible, but with the support and encouragement of so many, I feel less alone and more able to deliver something of value. Which is all I really aspire to do.

God bless you.

About the Author

Jim Donaher is a writer and blogger located in Eastern Massachusetts.

He grew up in his beloved Weymouth, Massachusetts playing sports, sweating out math classes, and attending Mass at Immaculate Conception Church every weekend.

He feels called to use his gifts to help others and contribute to the Lord's work in the world.

A fan of the Boston Celtics, and basset hounds, Jim lives in Walpole with his wife Gina.

References

[i]The Trinity - UnderstandChristianity.com ©2021

[ii]https://worldeventsandthebible.com/wp-content/uploads/2017/02/Cattle-Yoke.png

[iii] KC Hairston, *The Forgotten Rules of Prayer.* (Downers Grove, IL: IVP Books), ©2004.